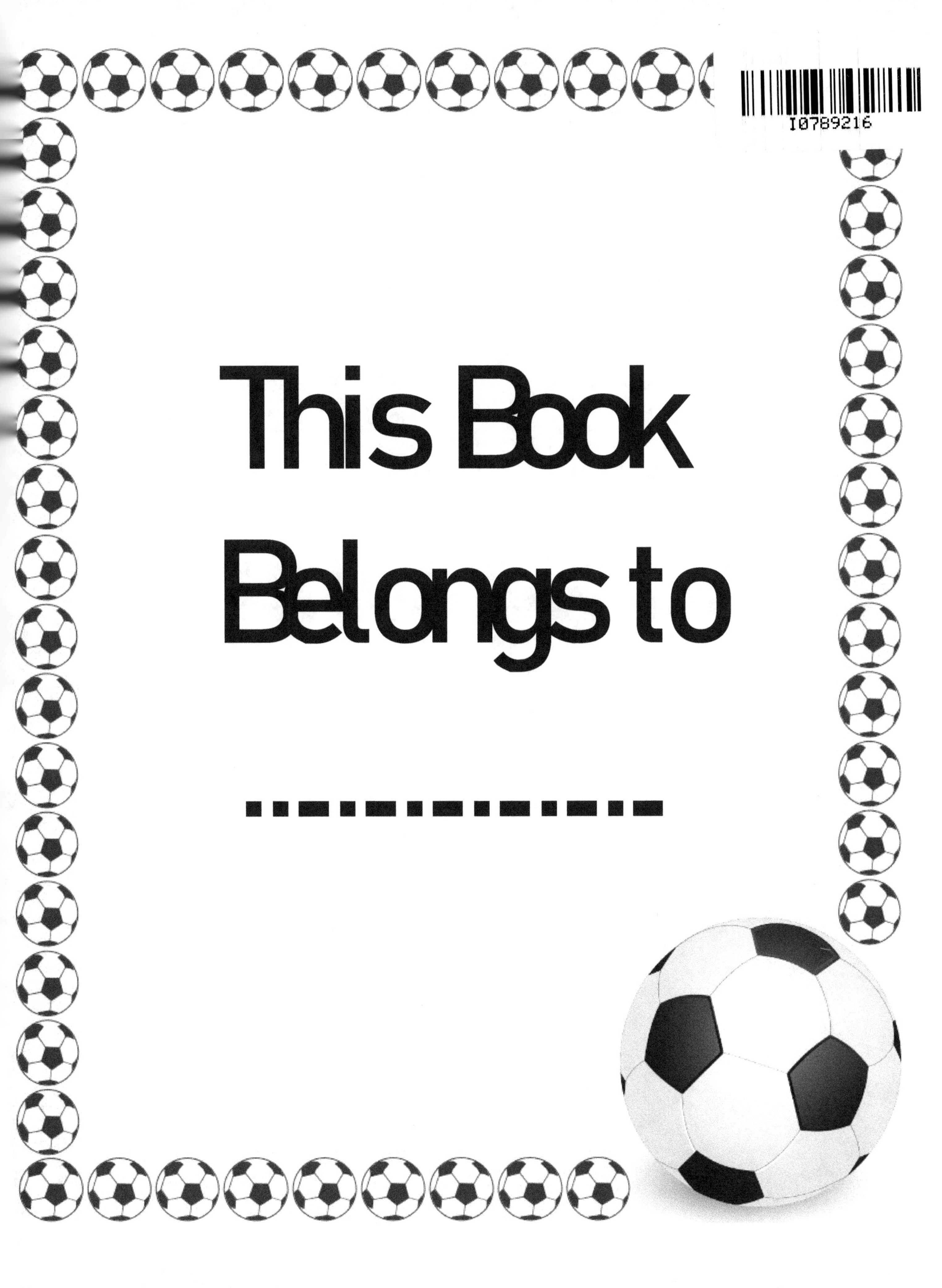

This Book
Belongs to
....

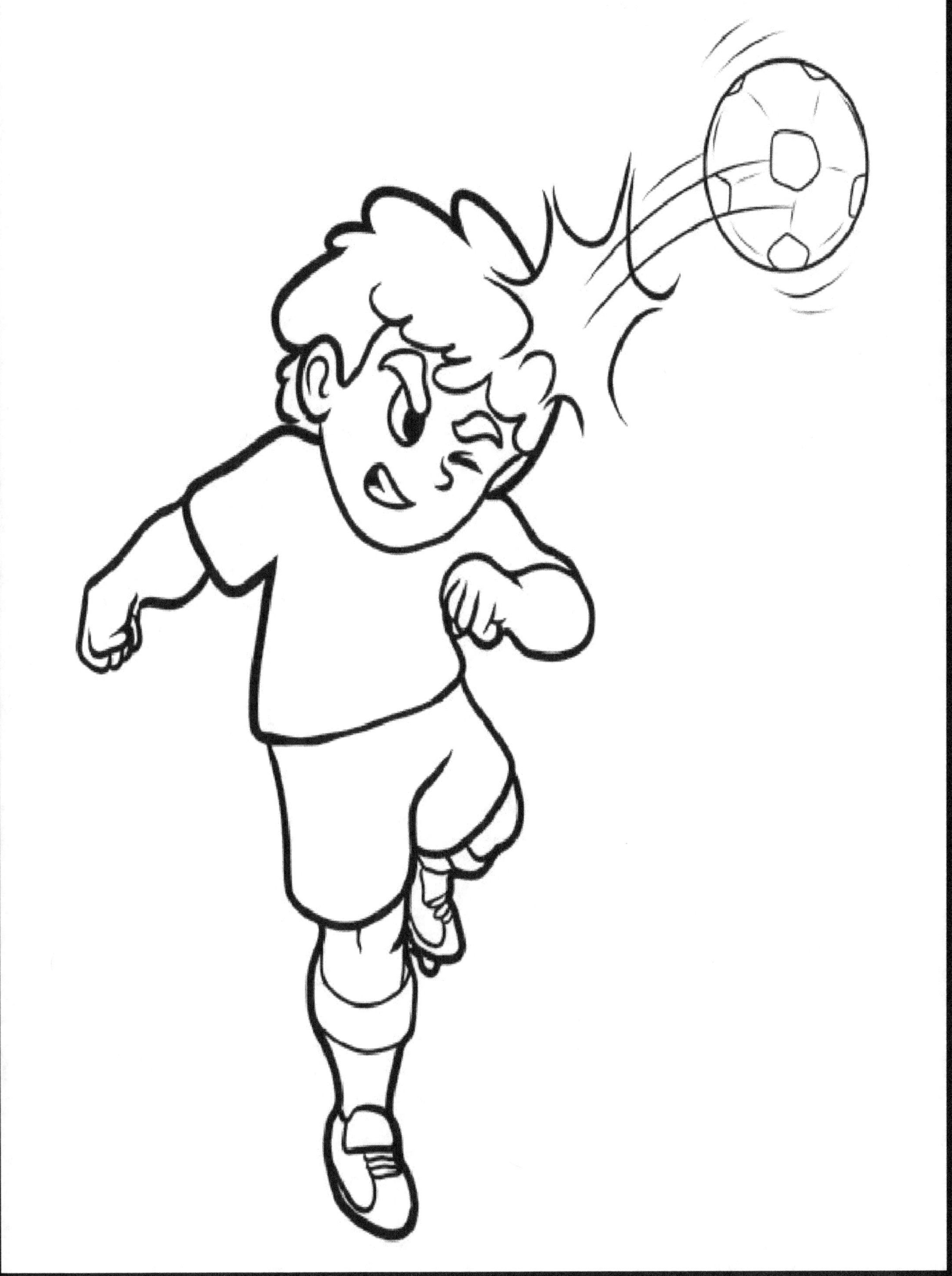

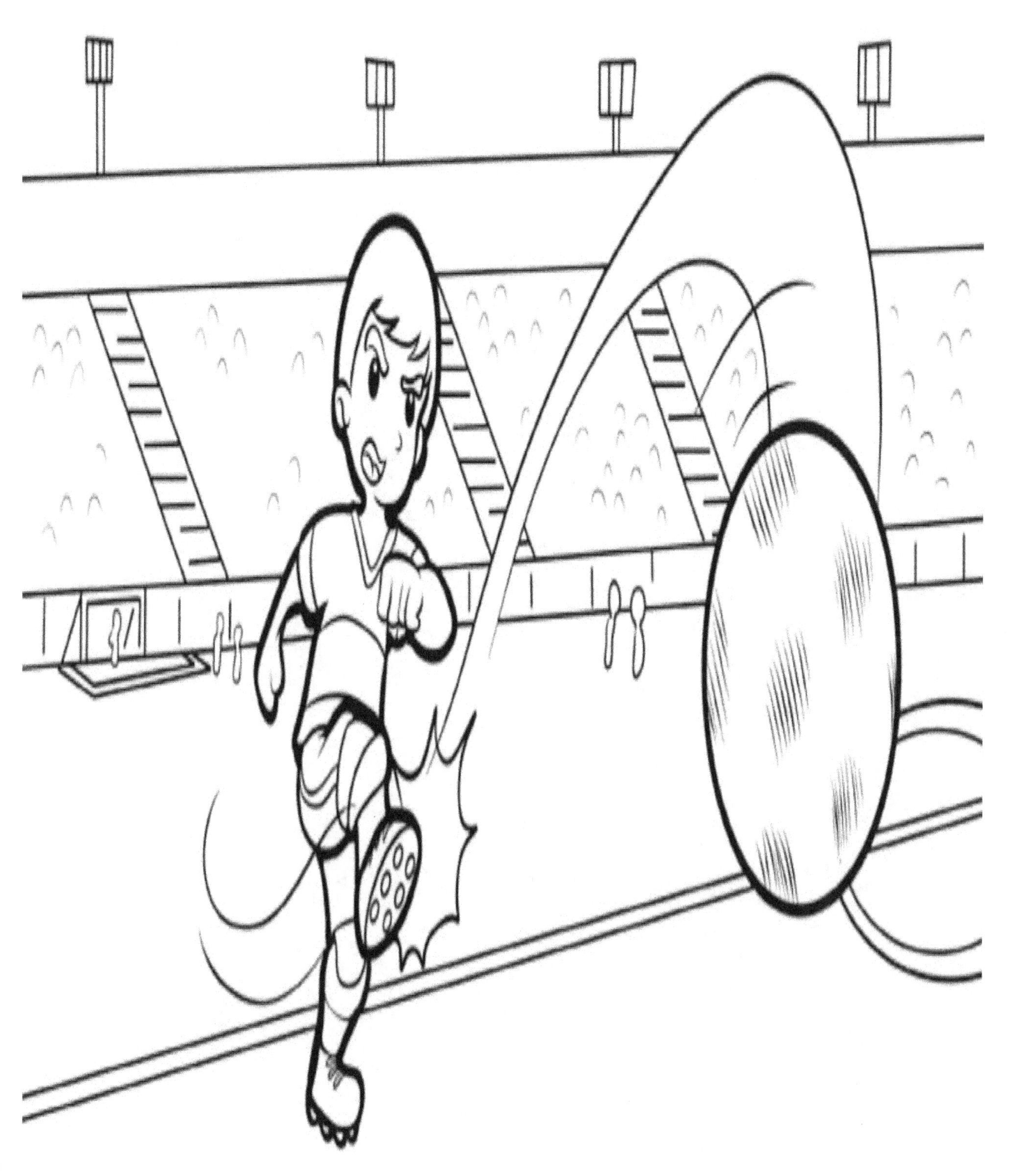

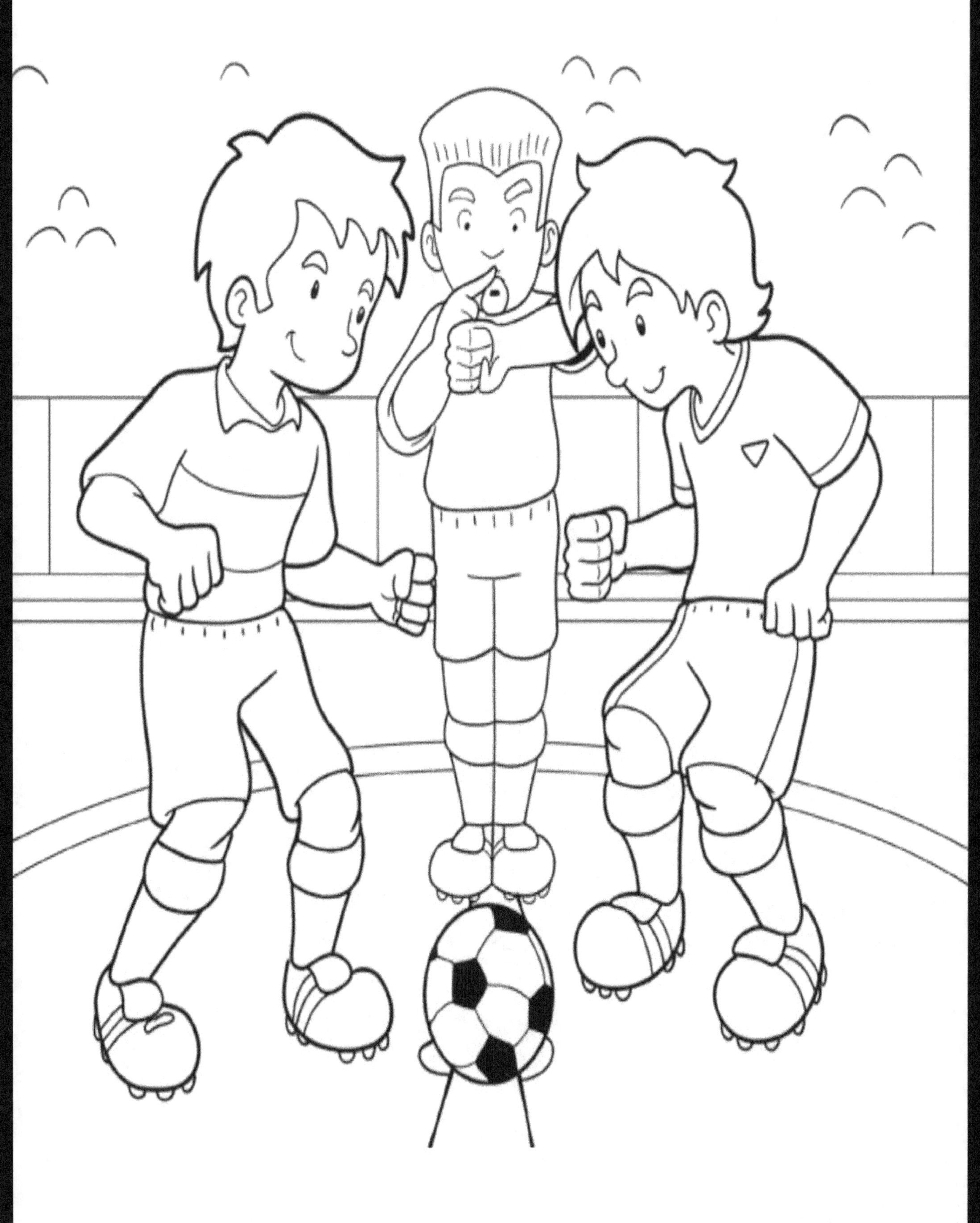

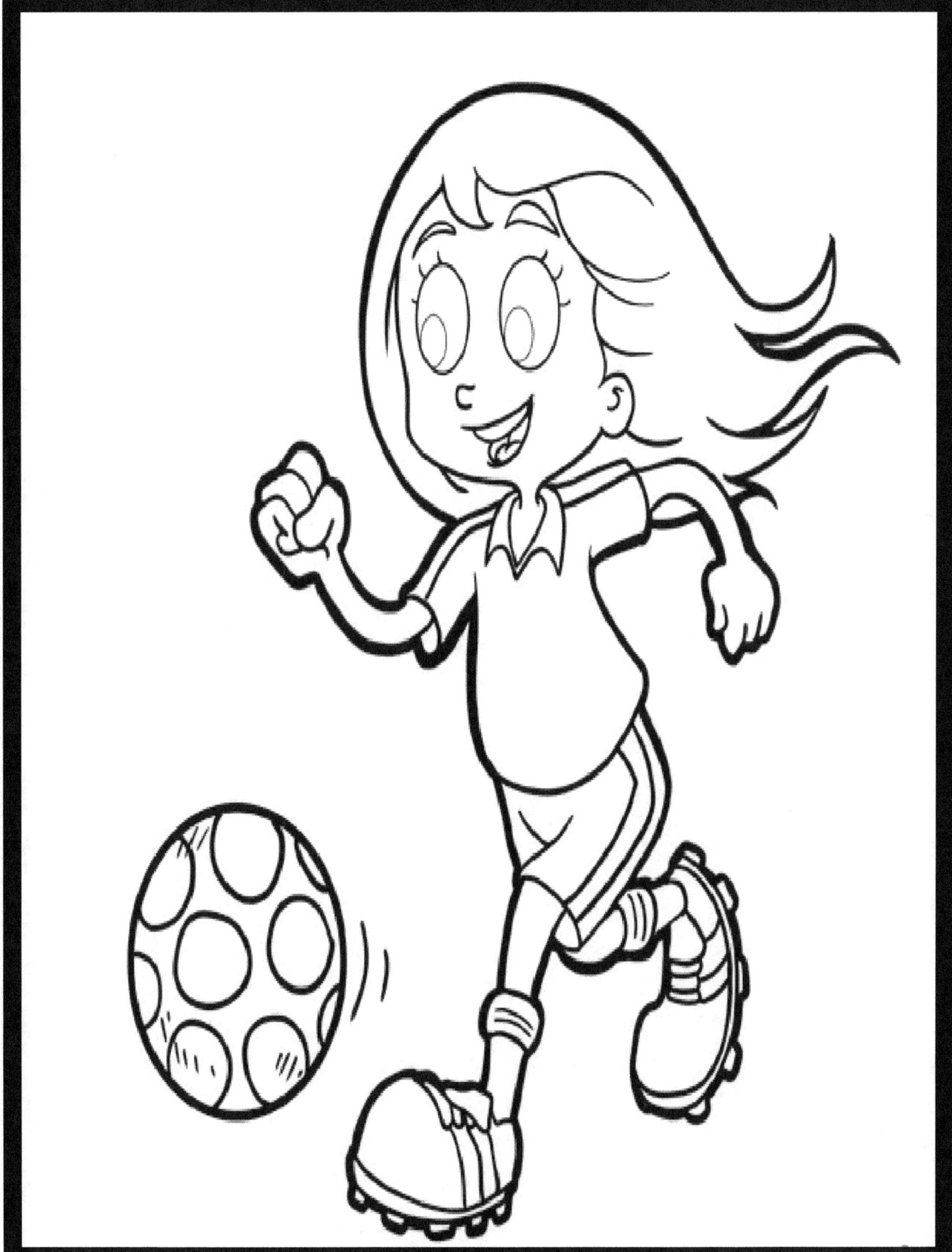

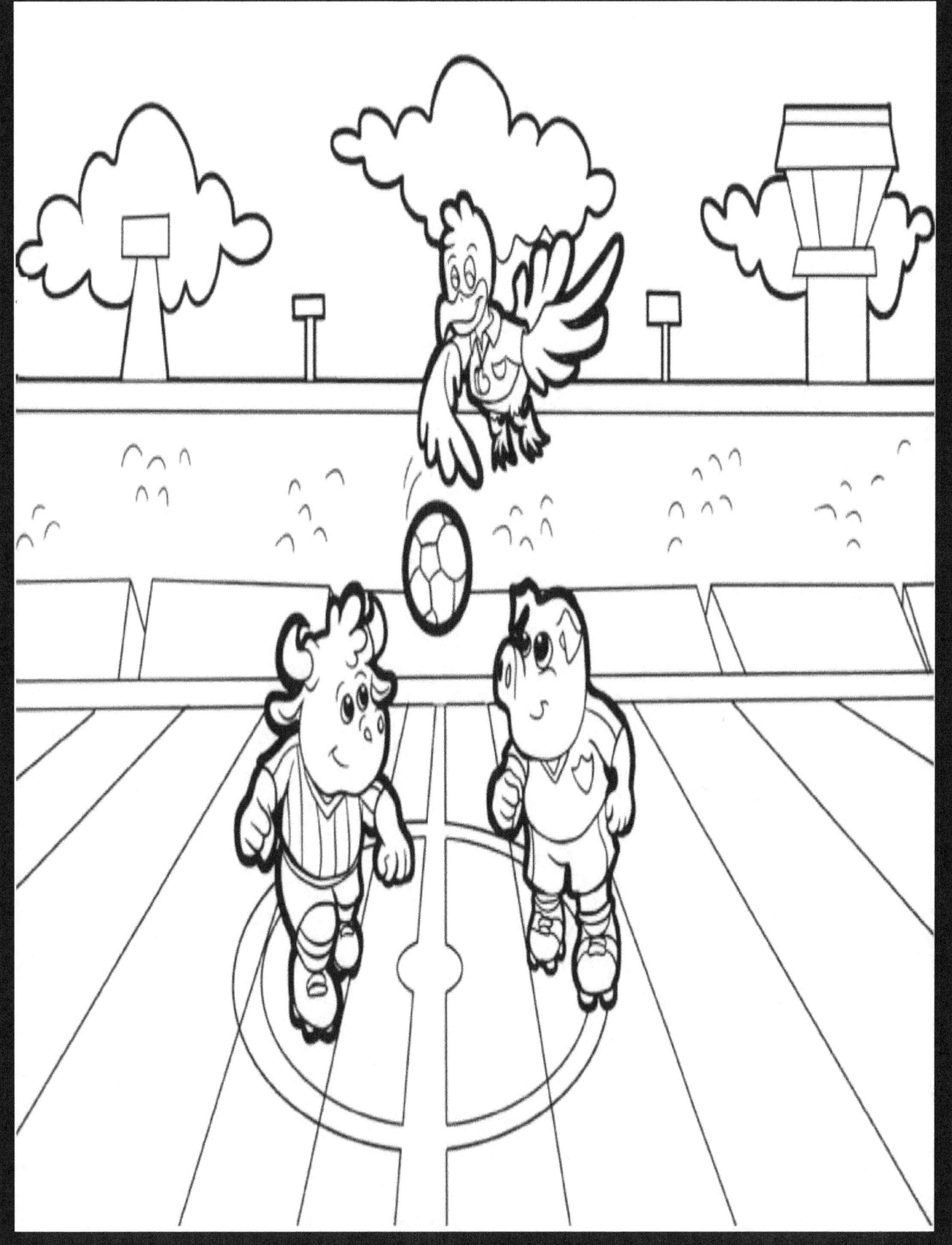

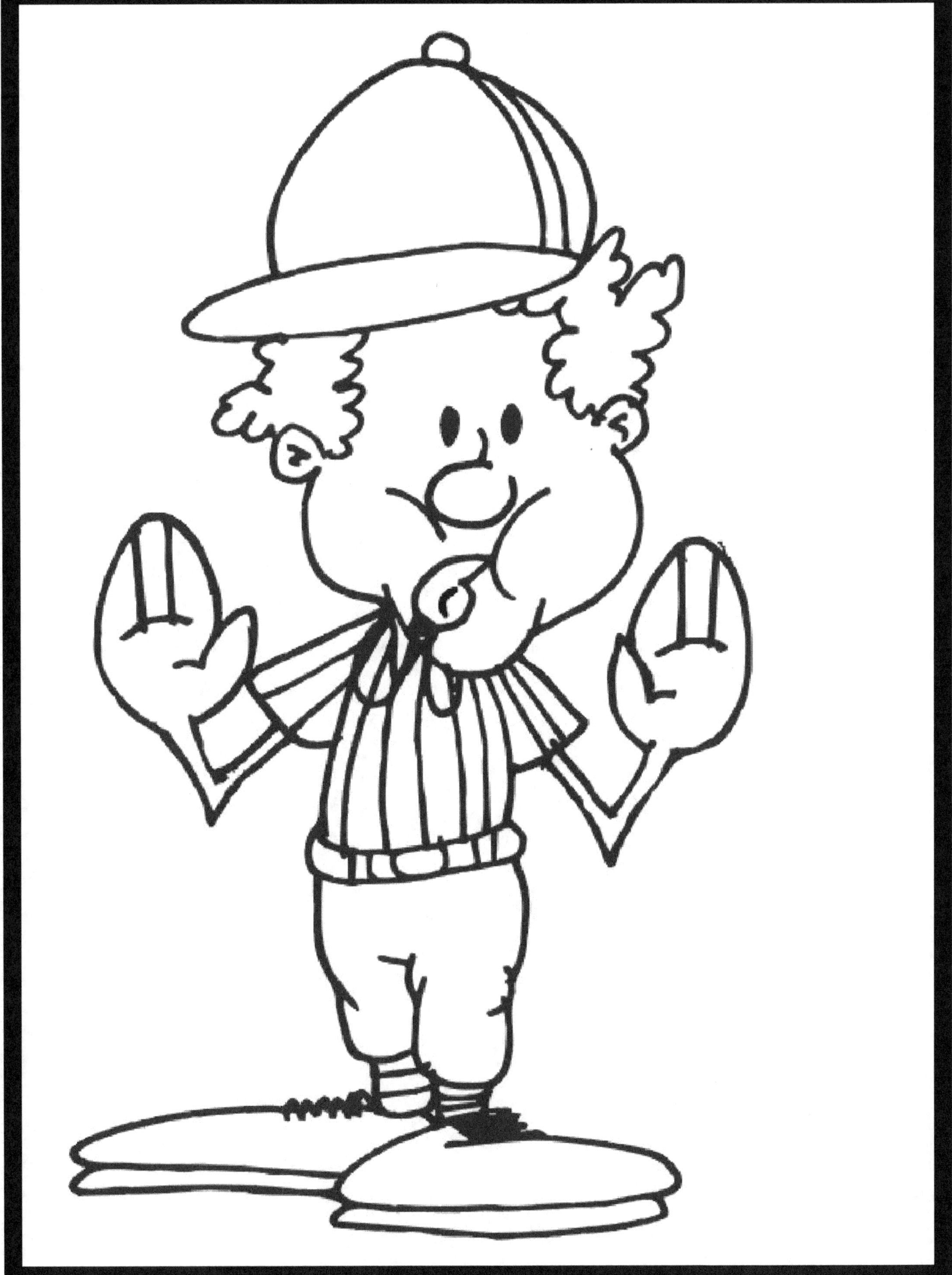

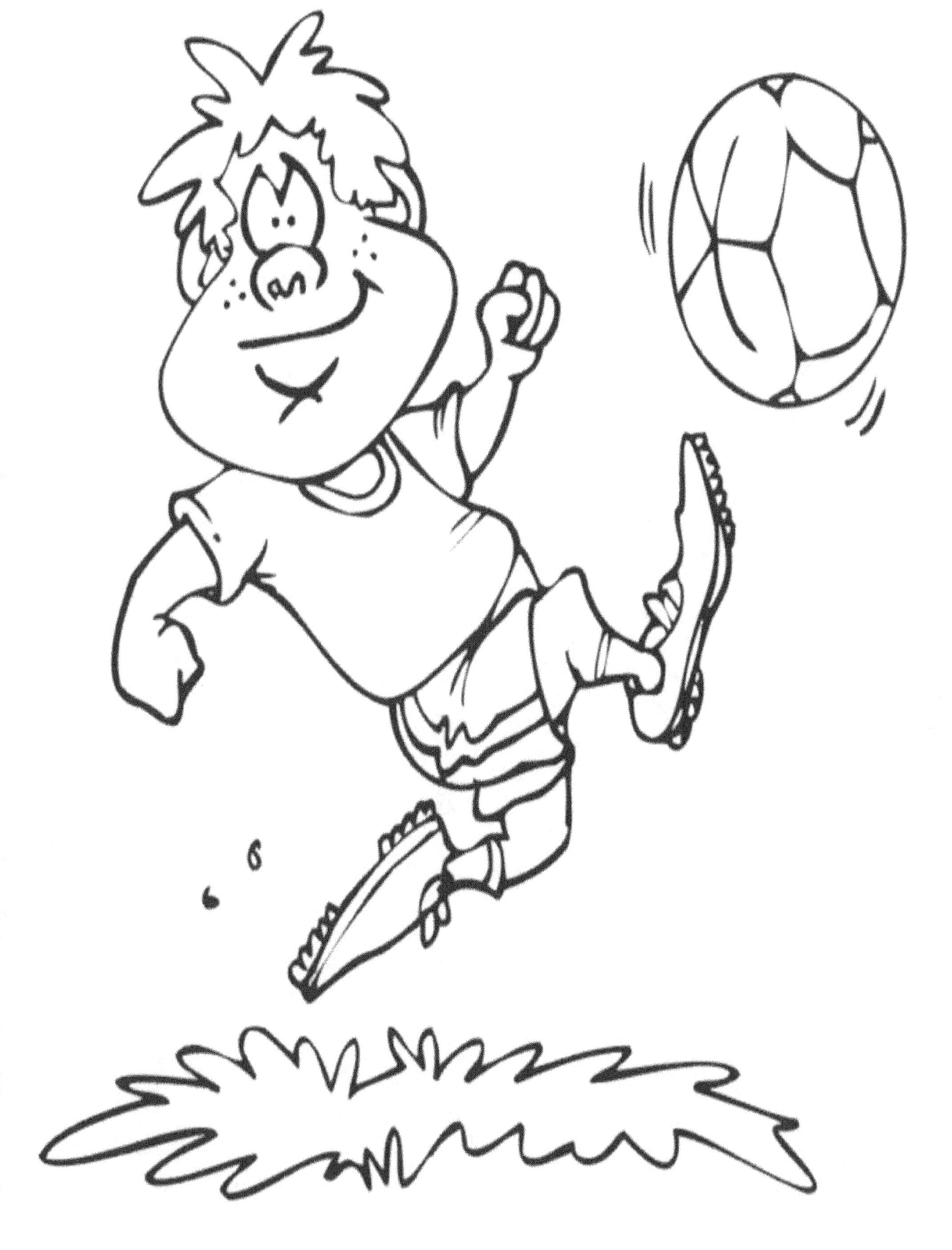

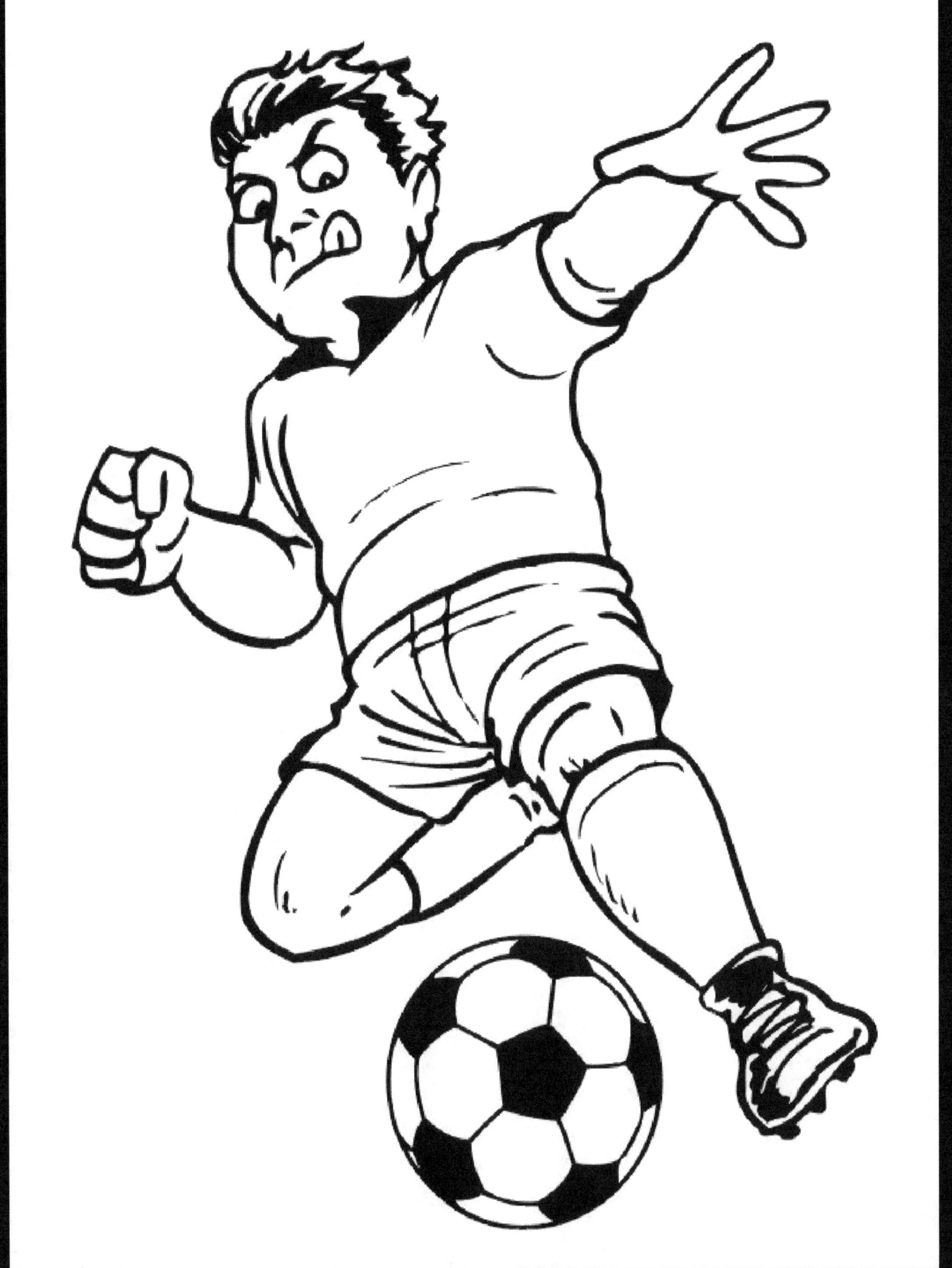

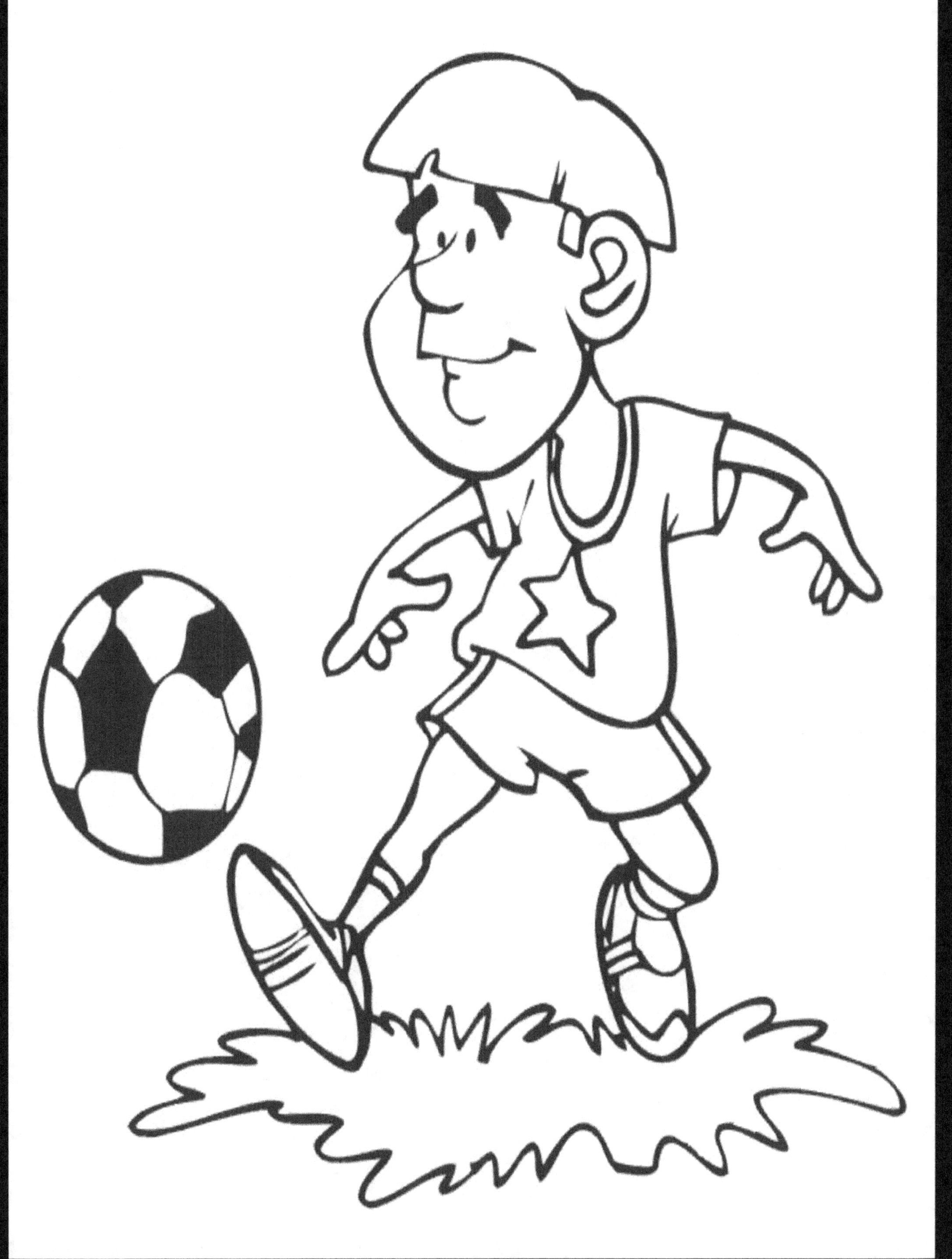

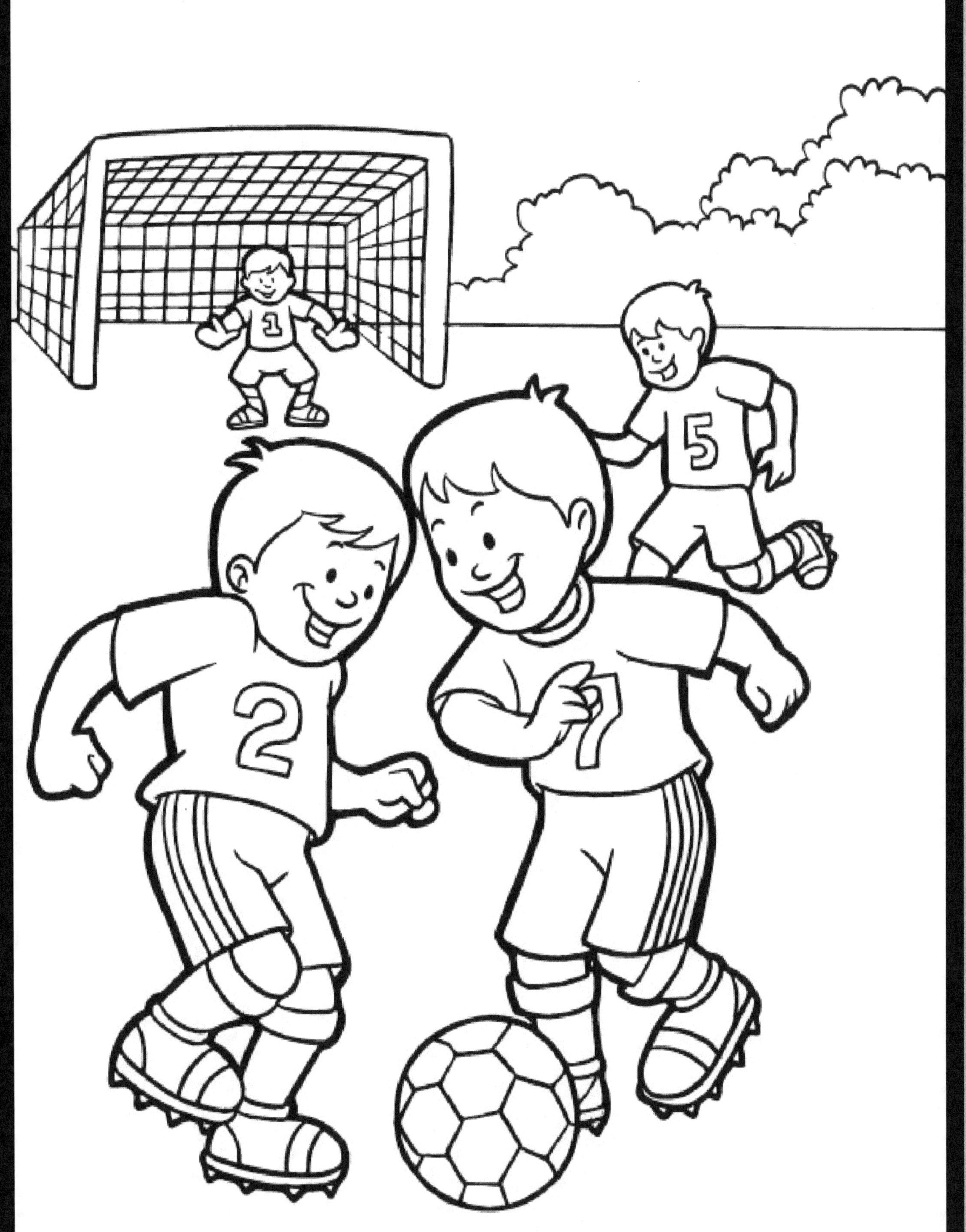

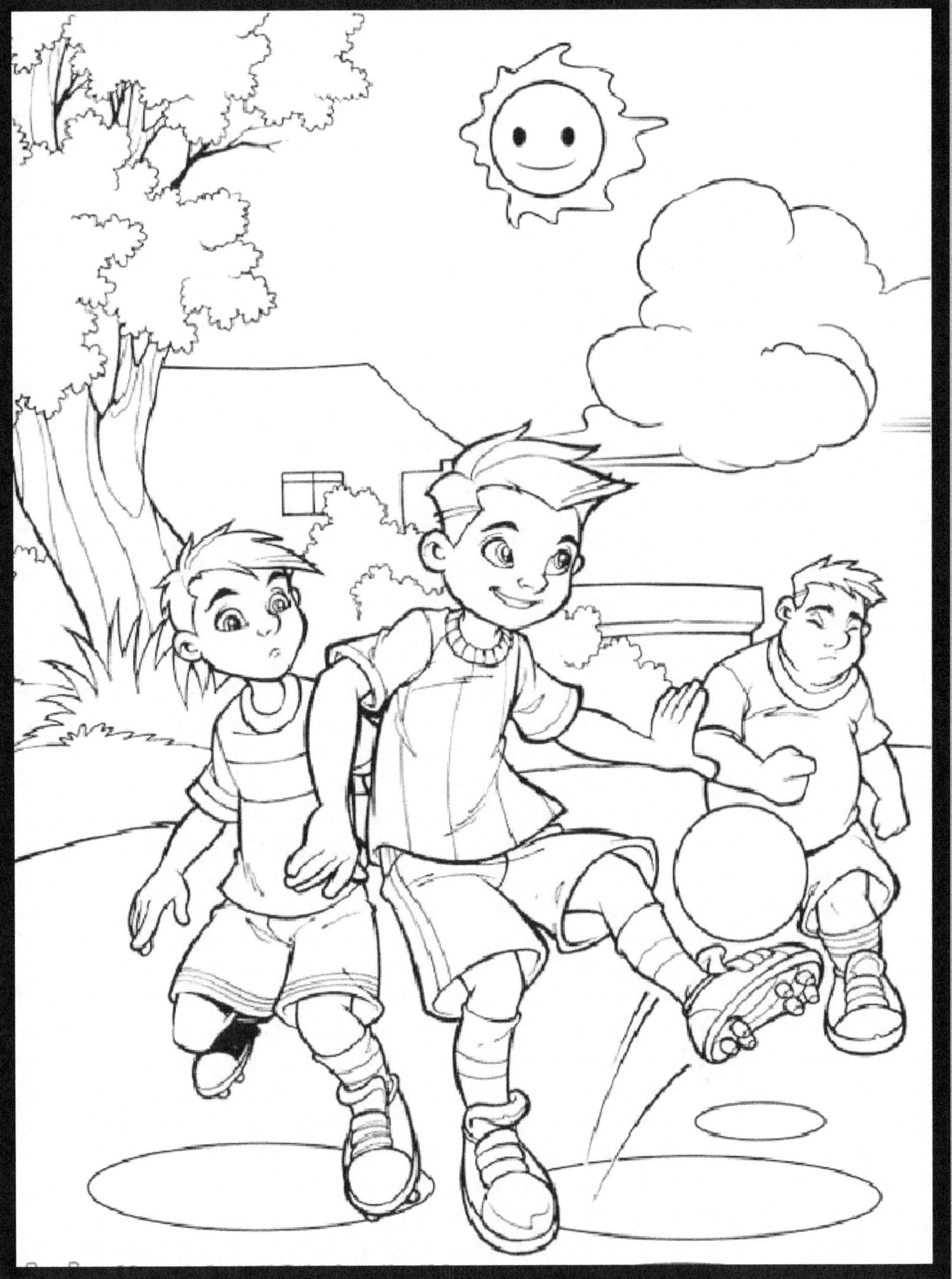

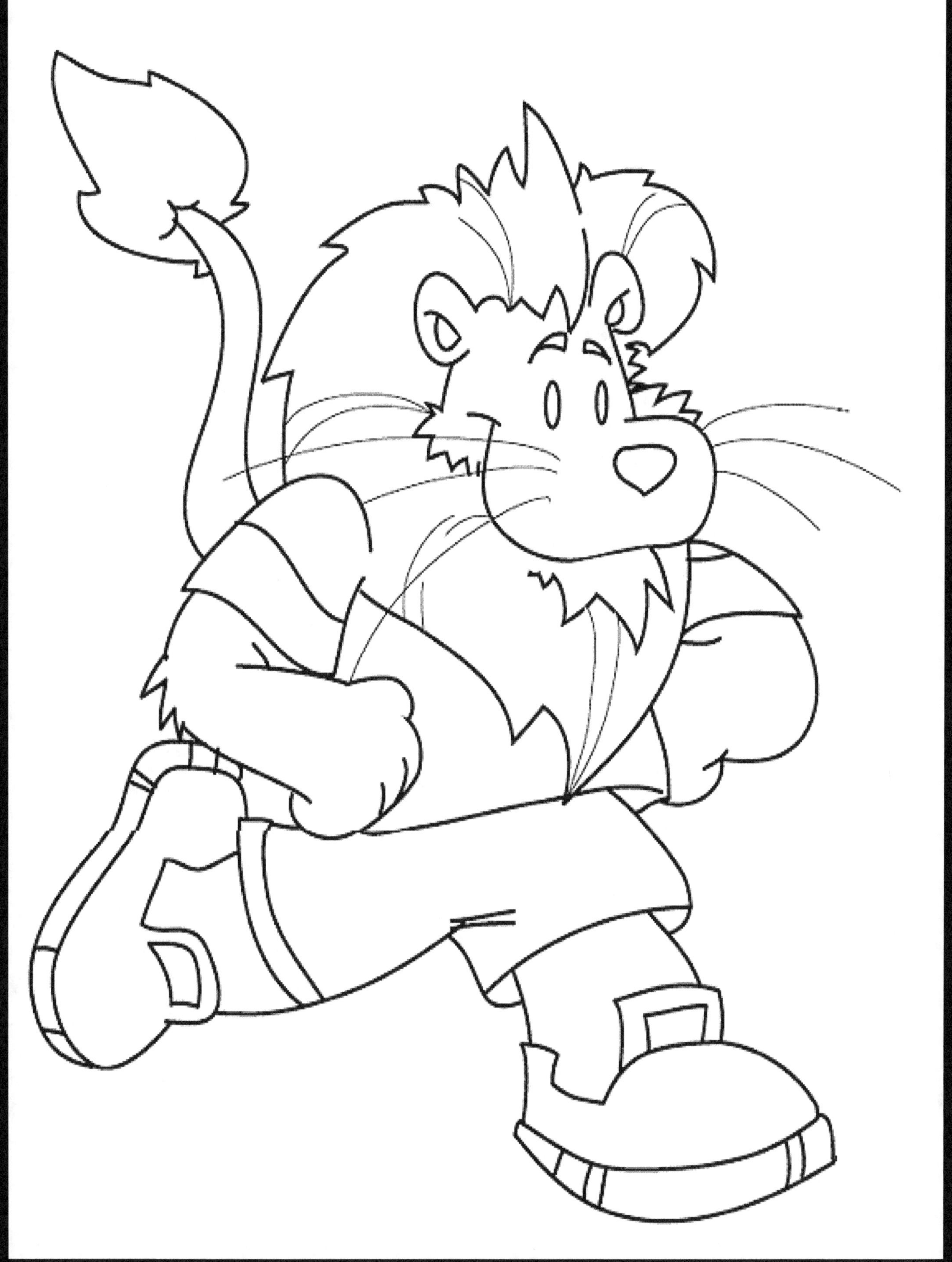

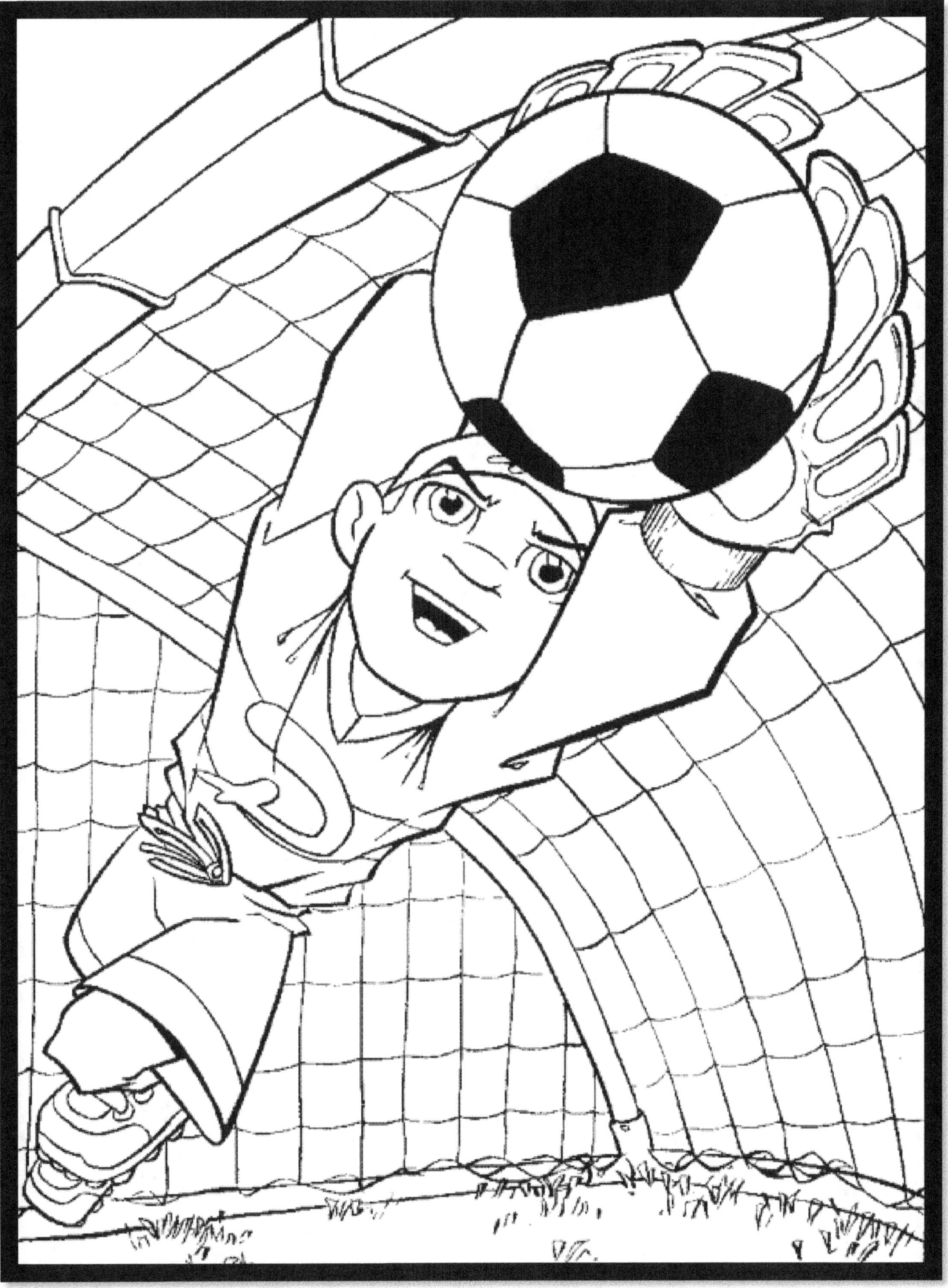

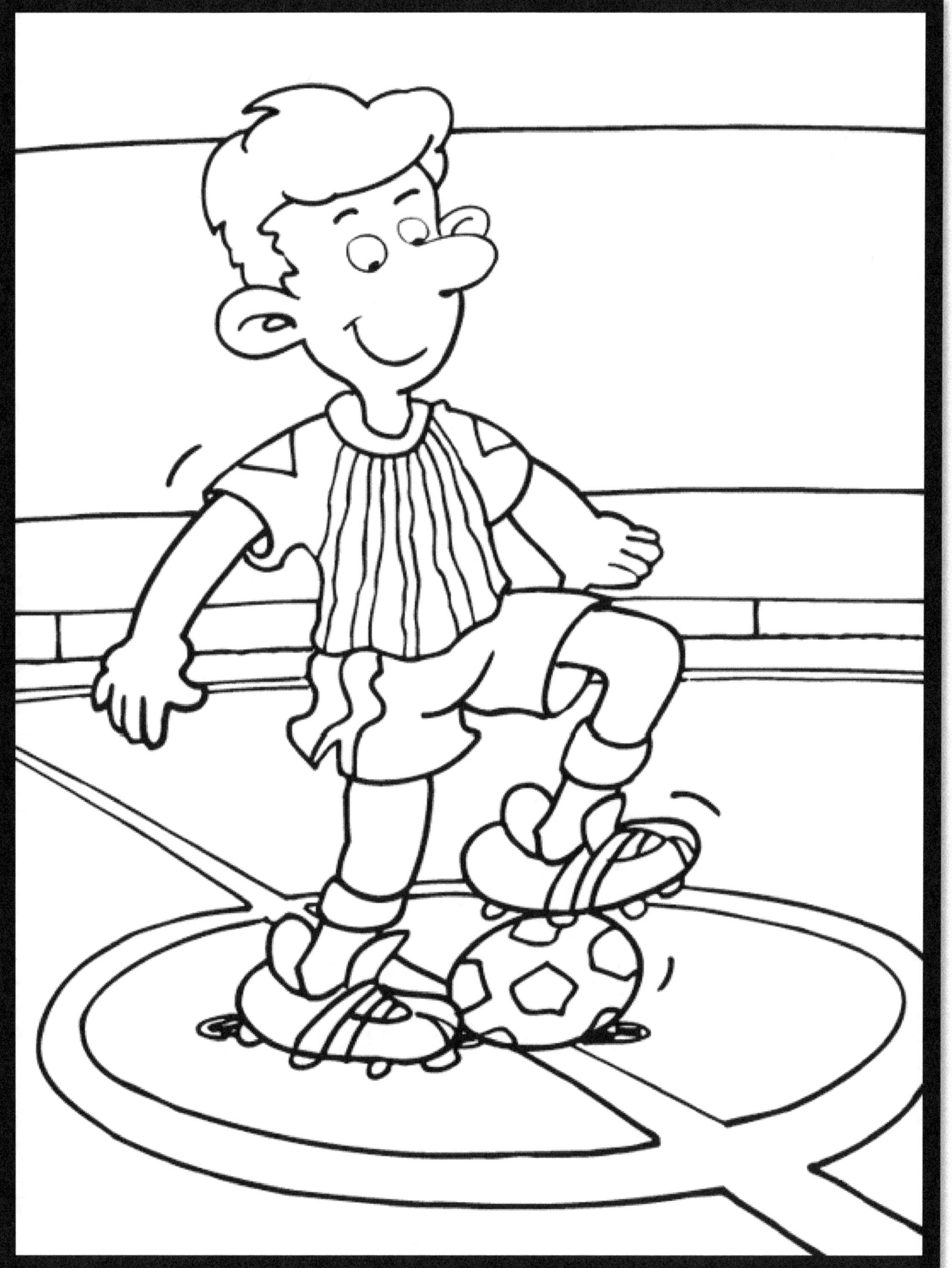

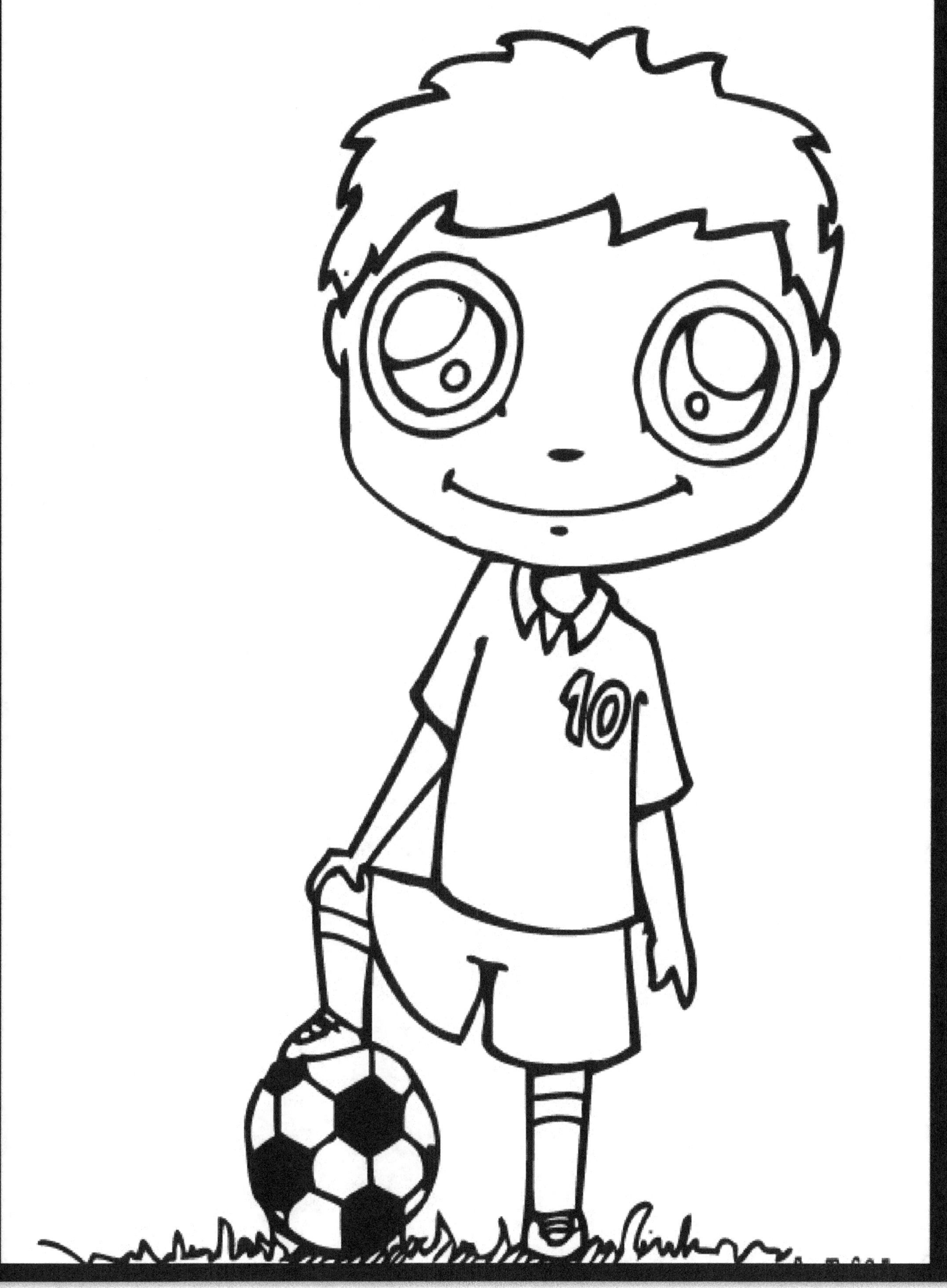

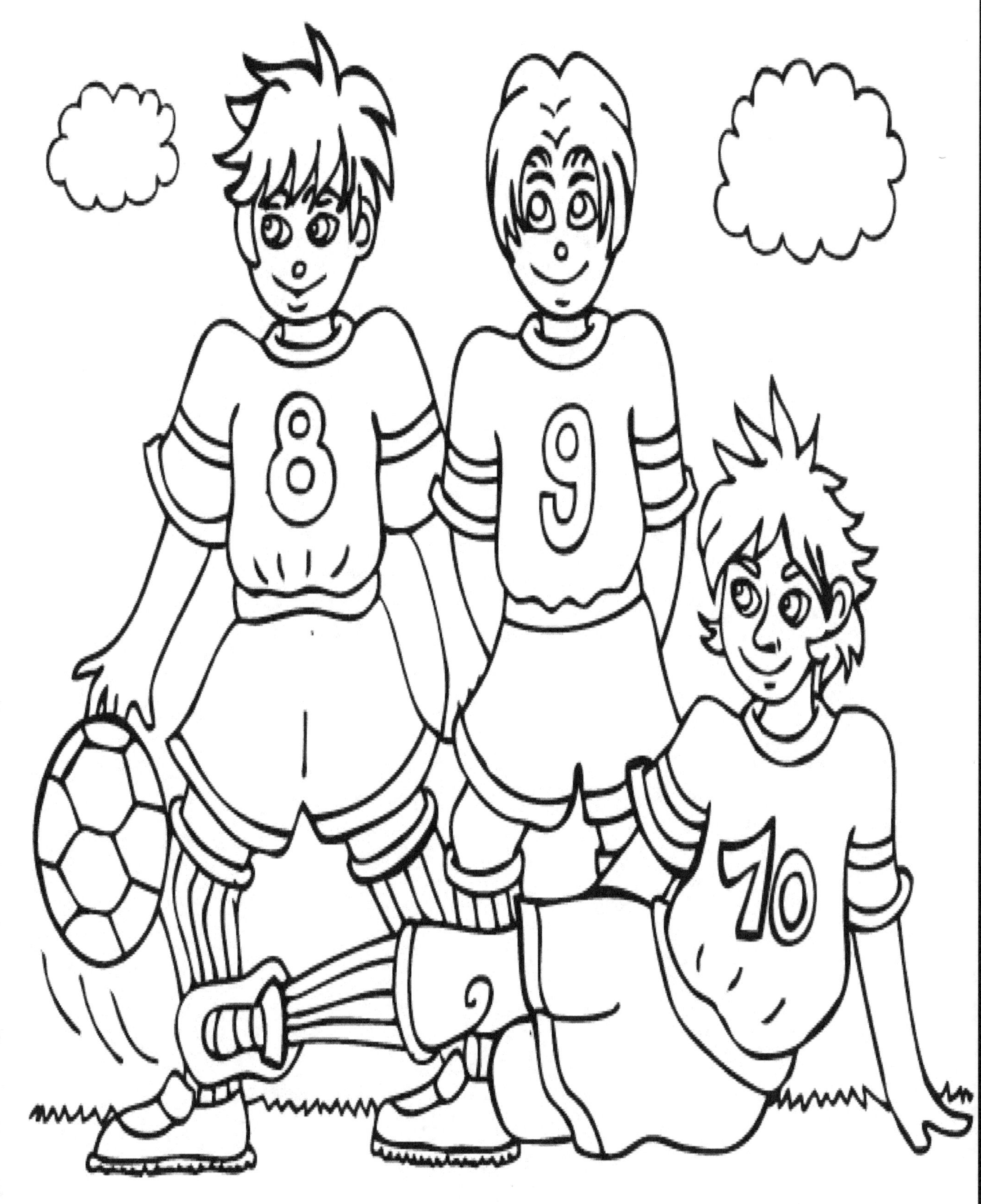

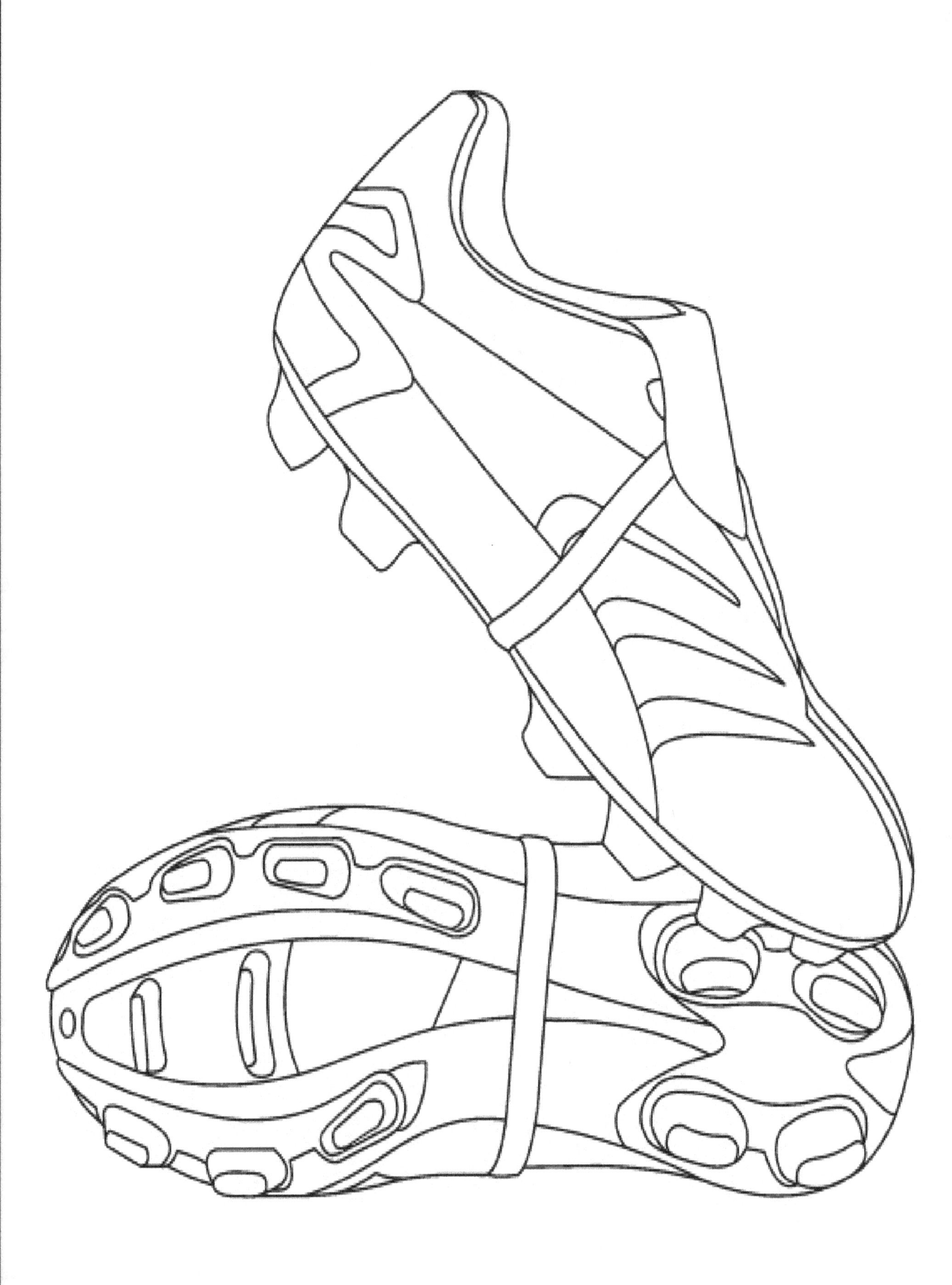

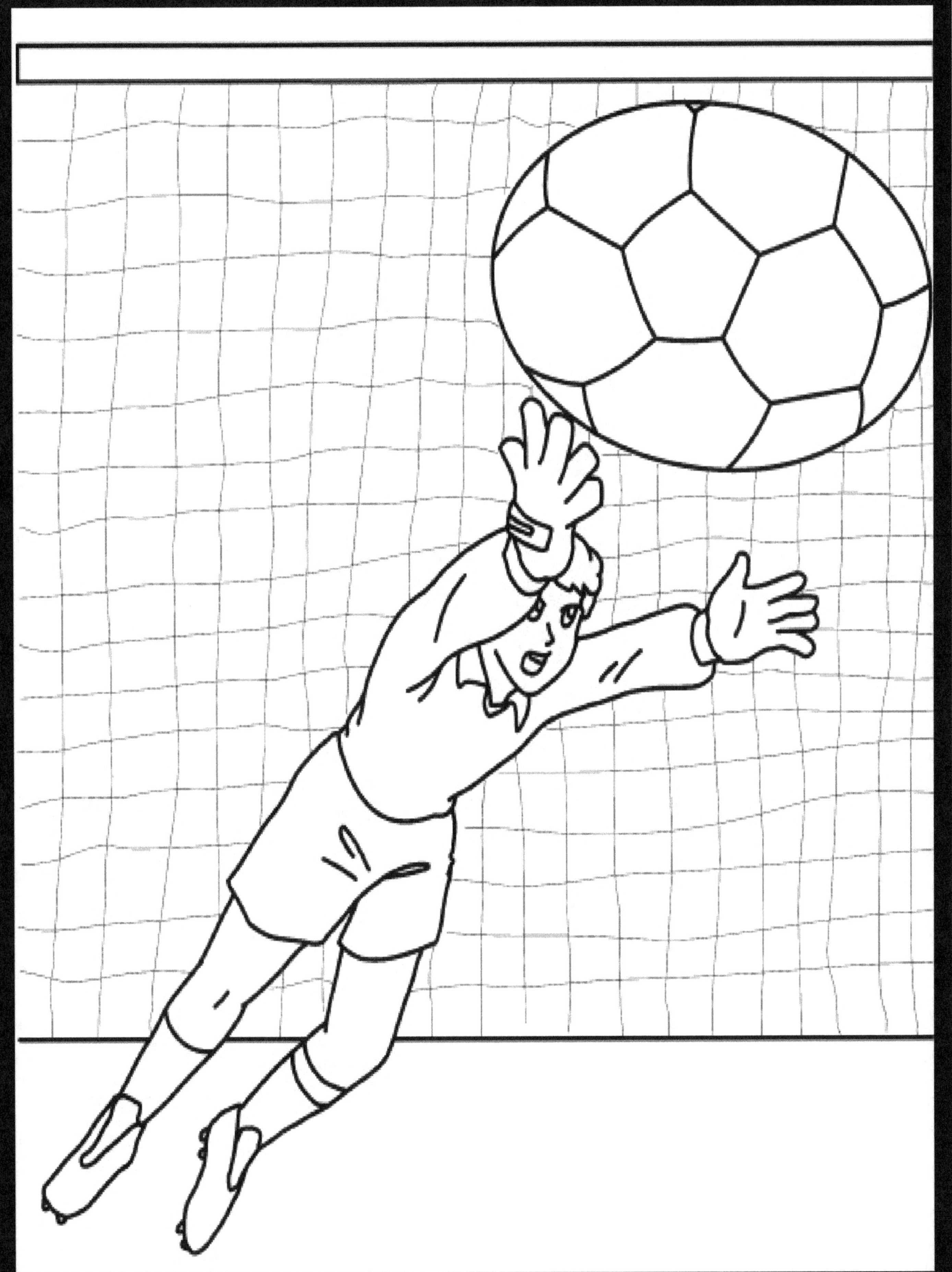

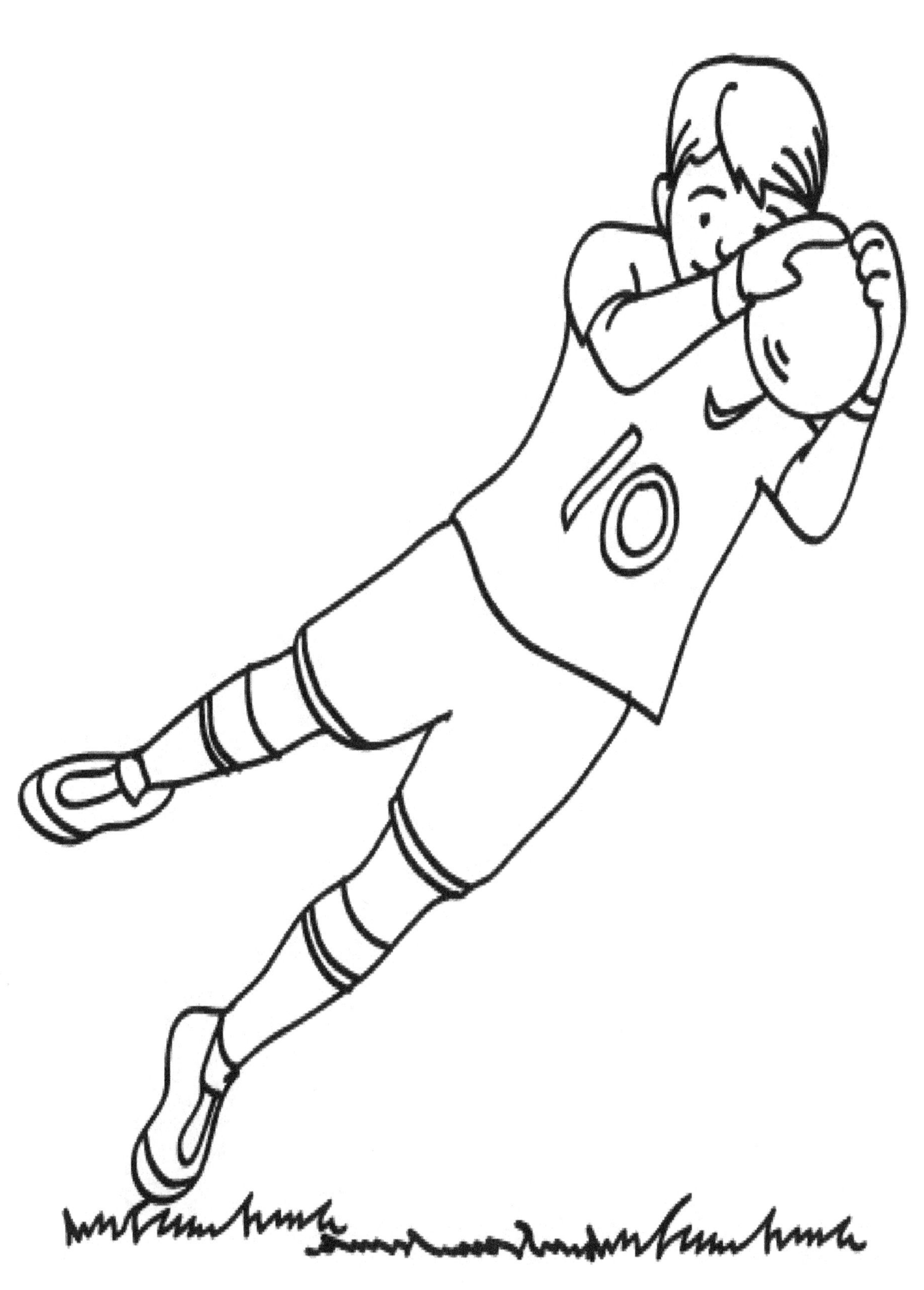

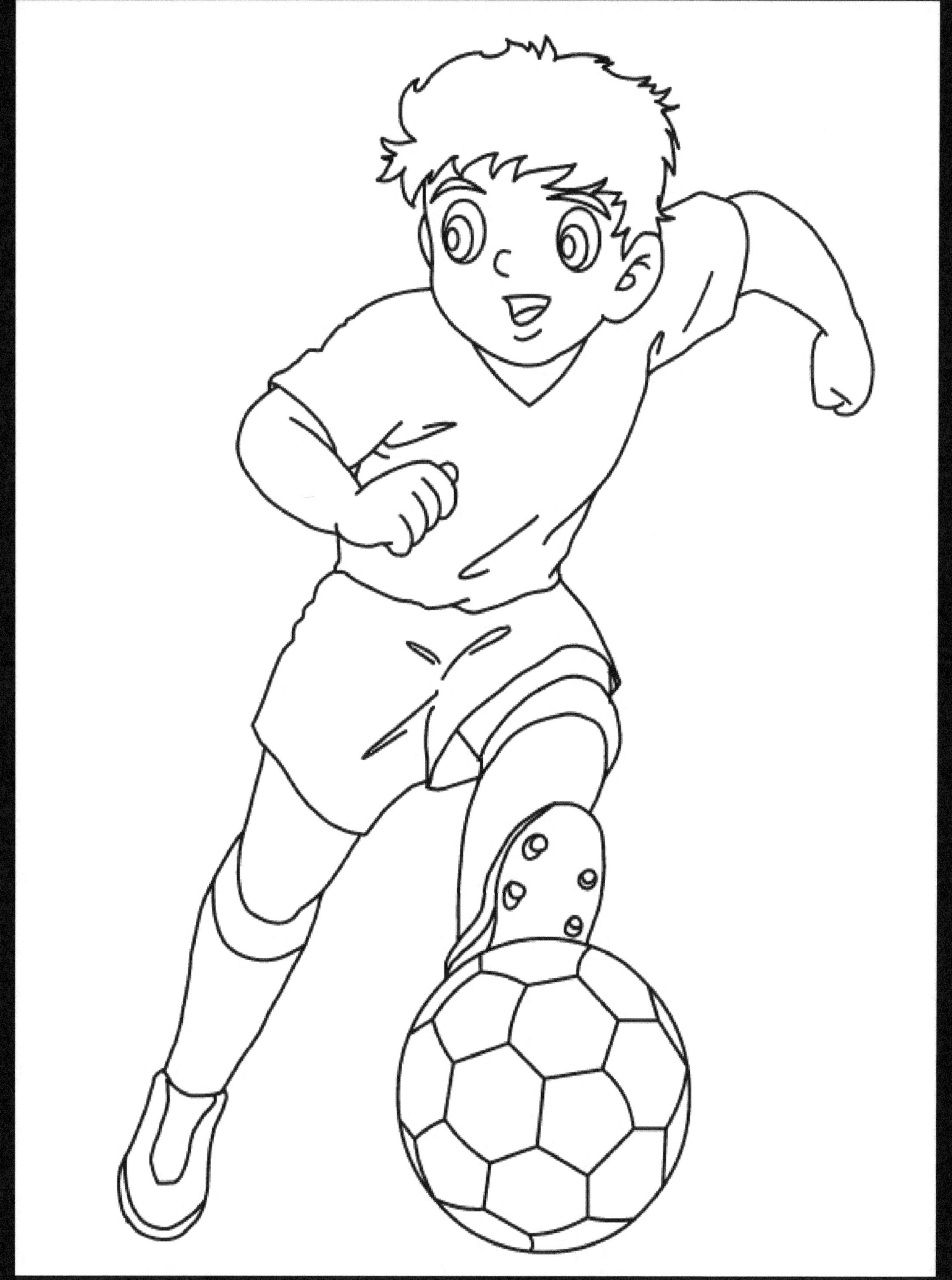

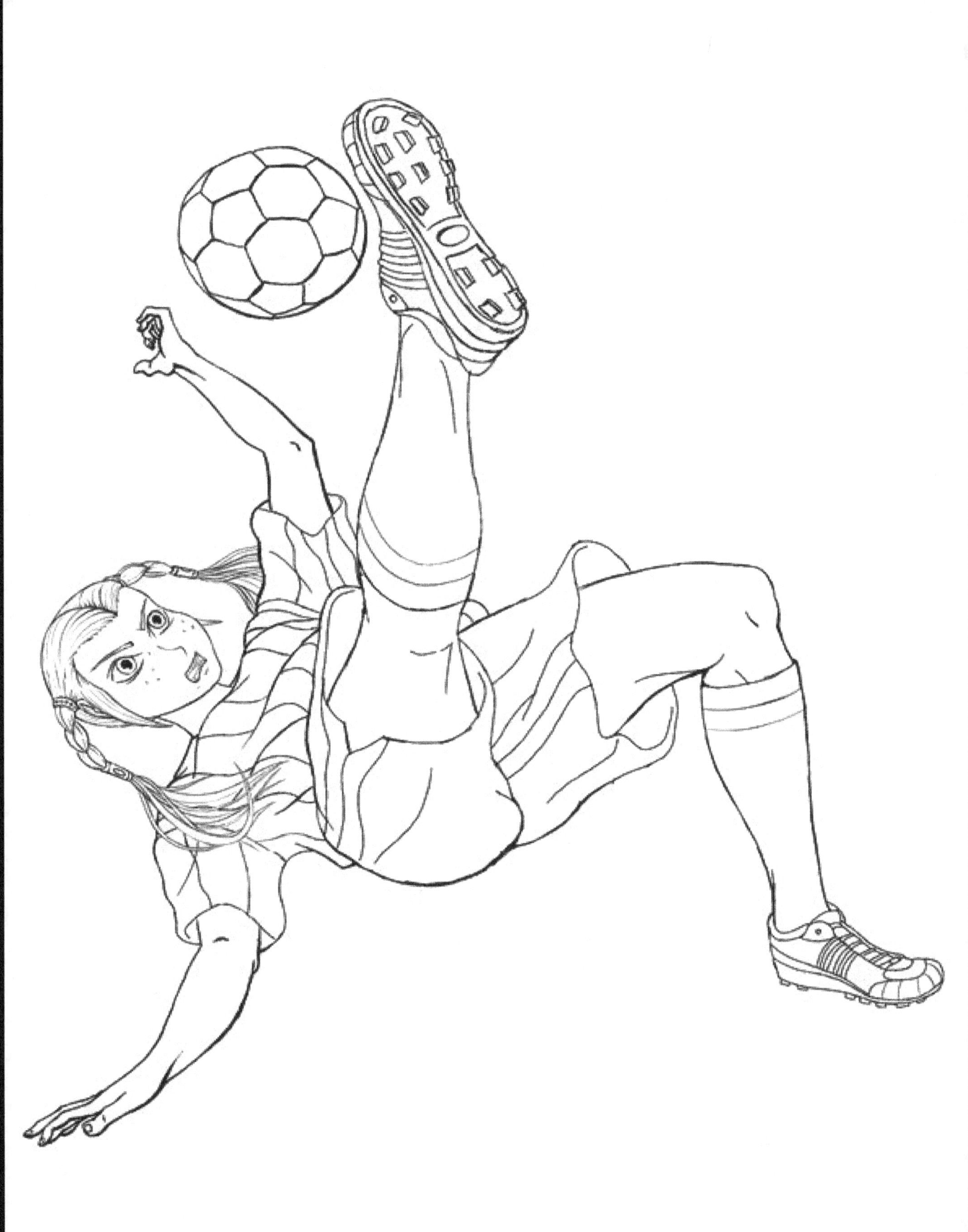

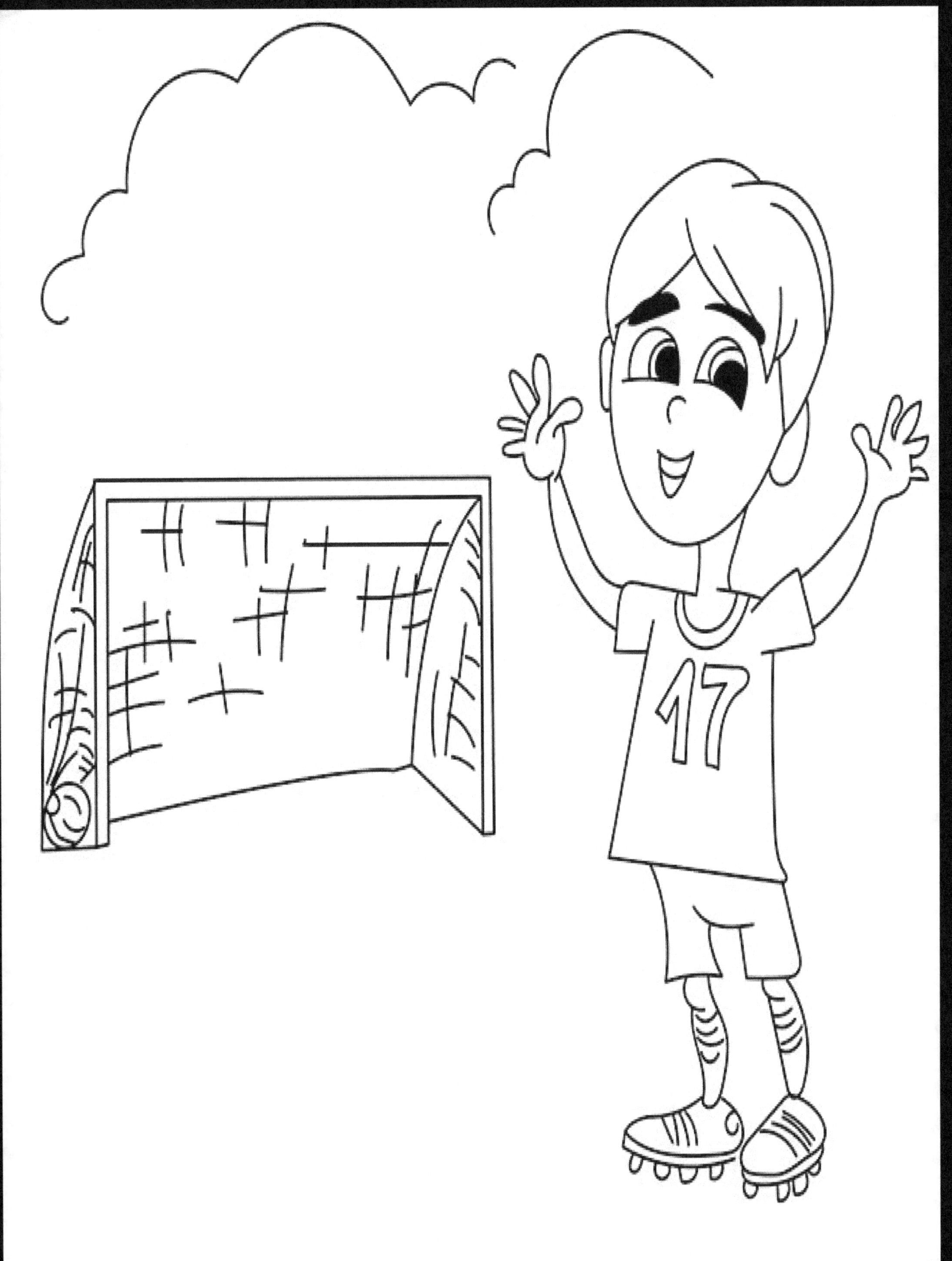
17

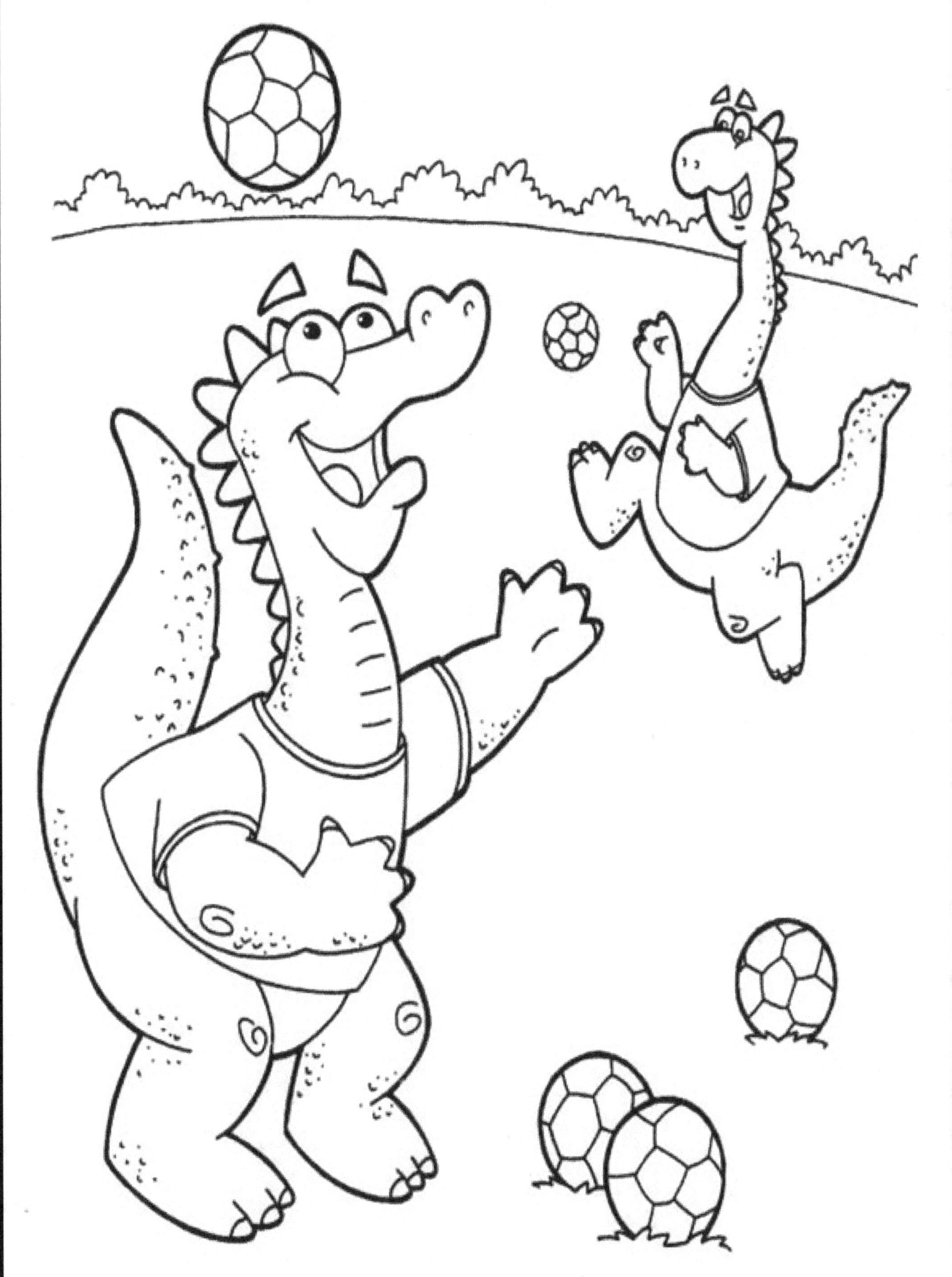

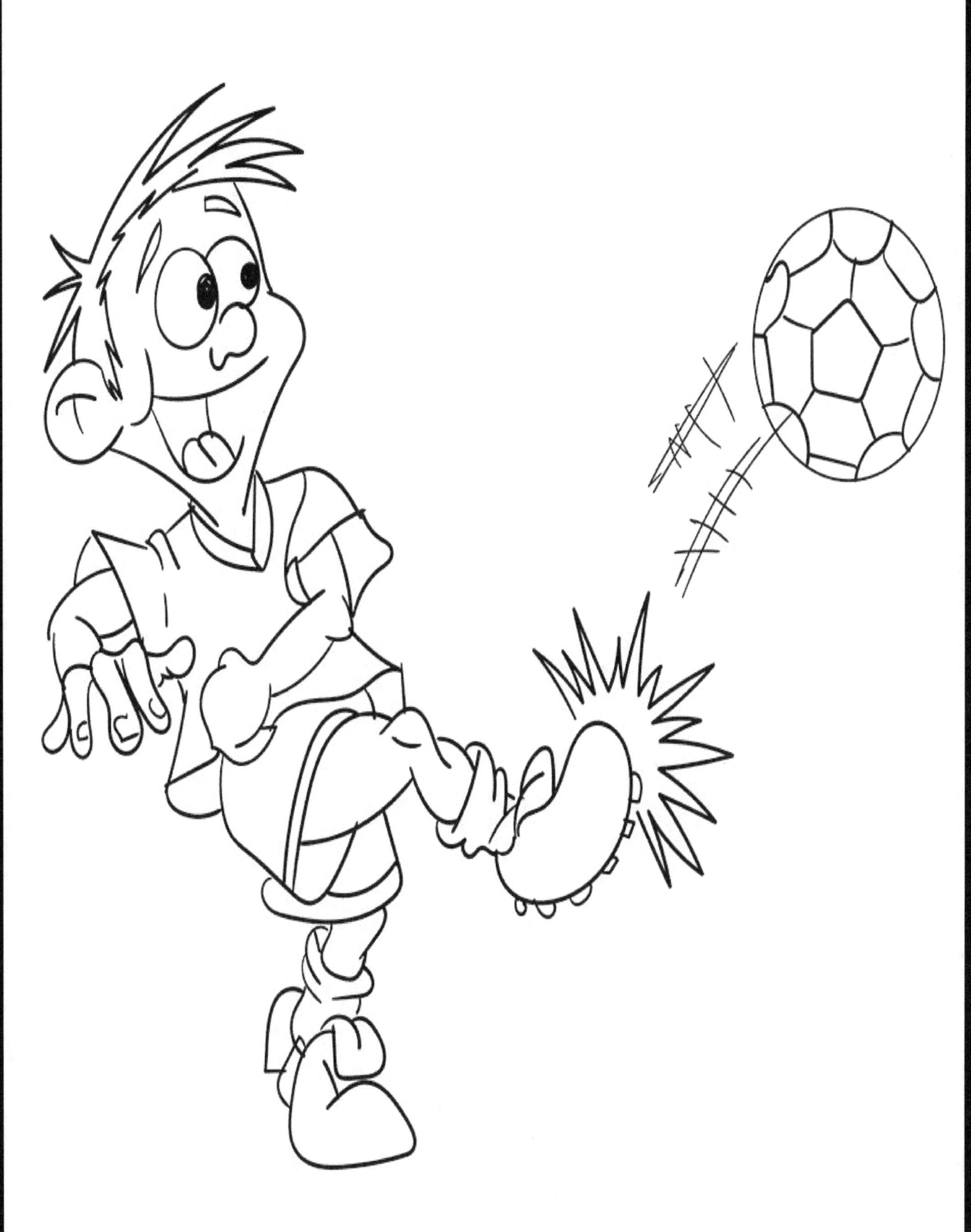

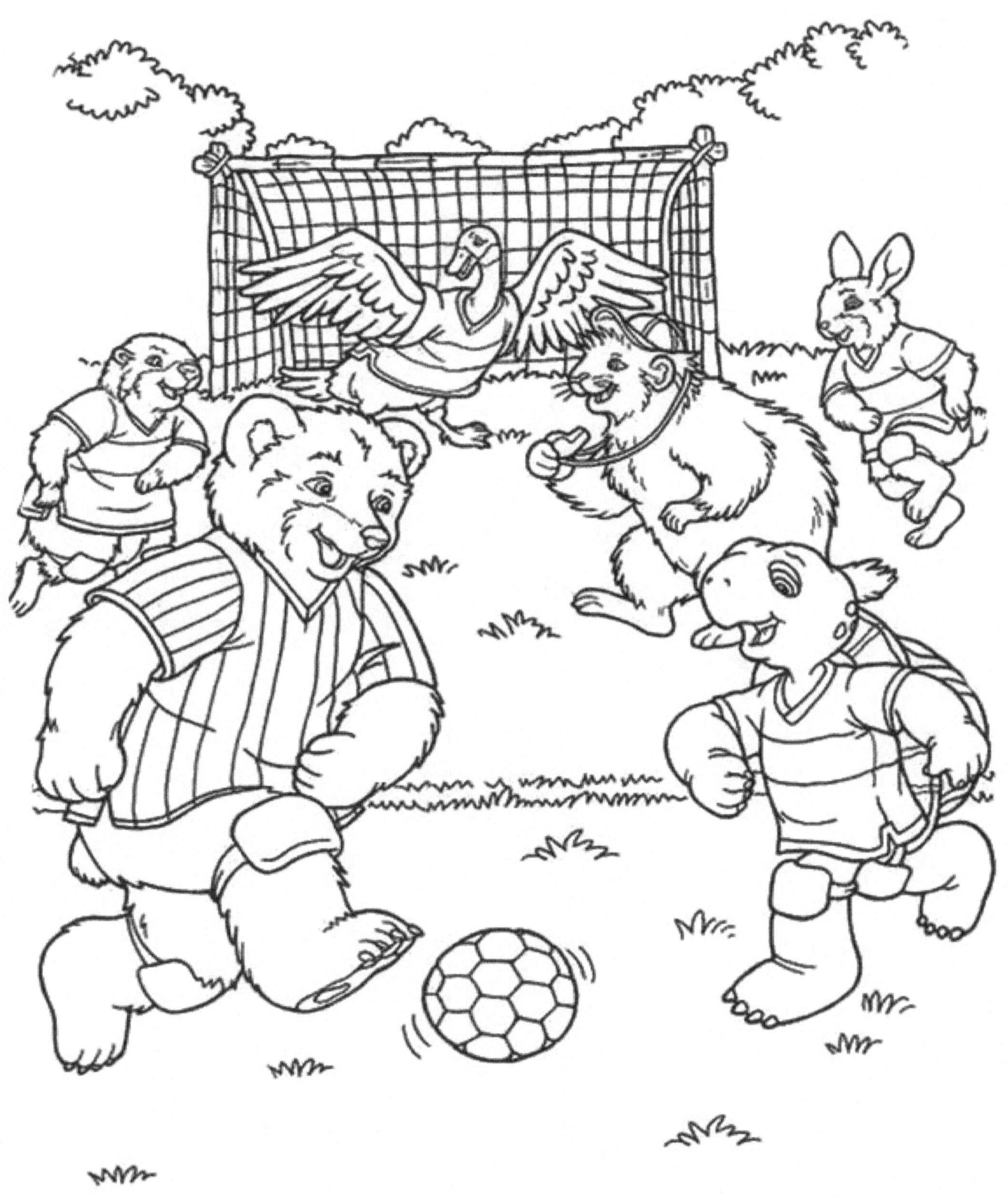

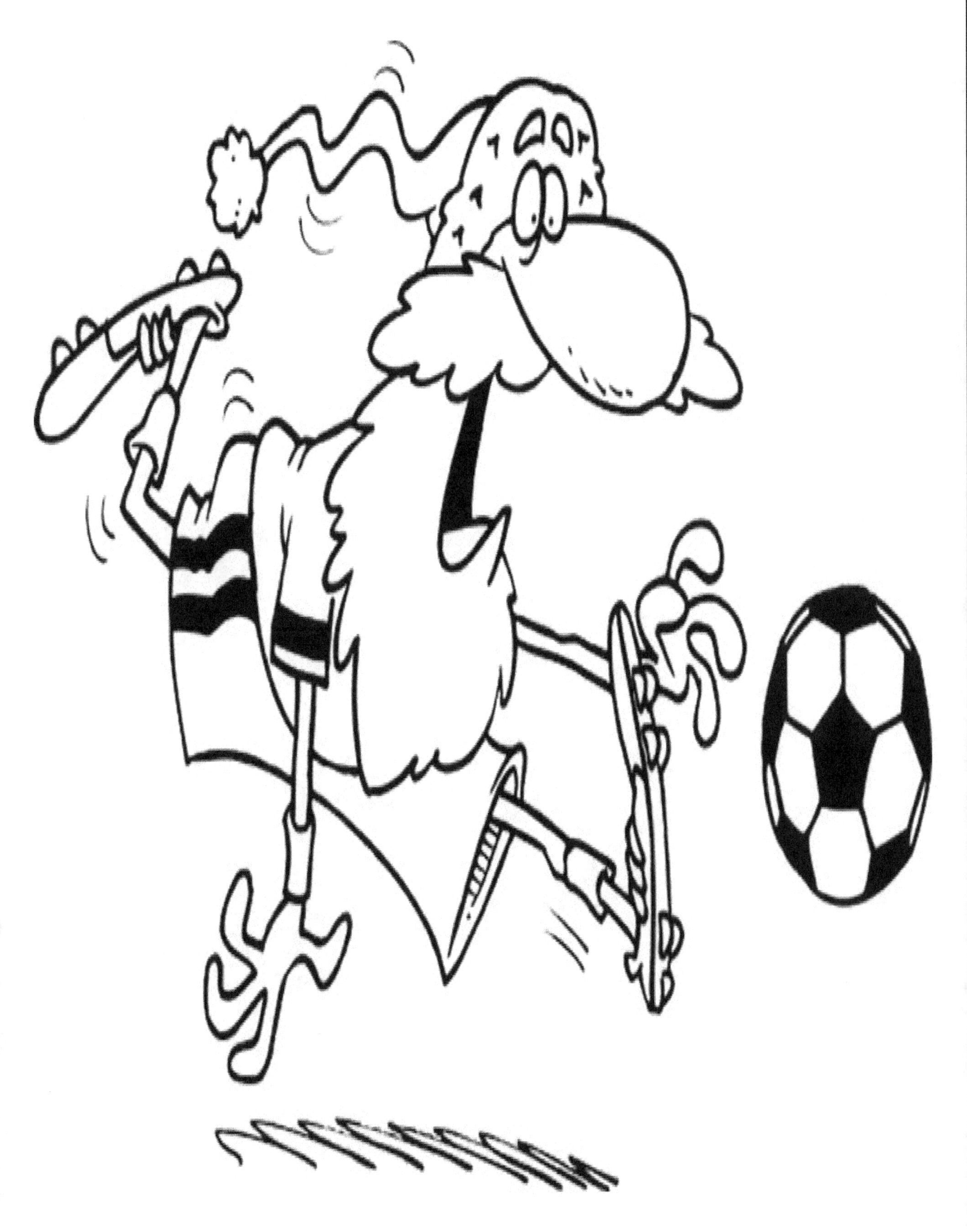

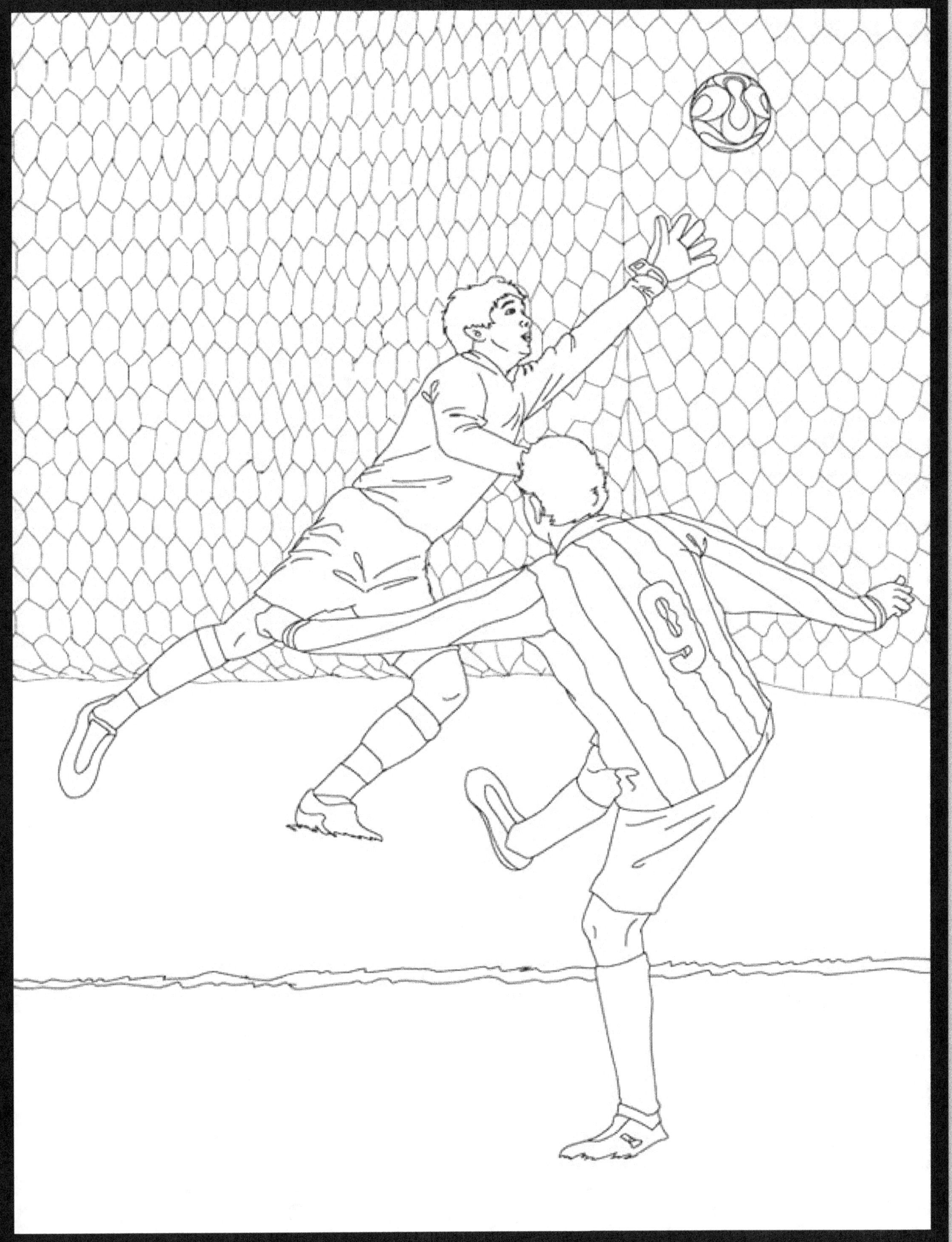

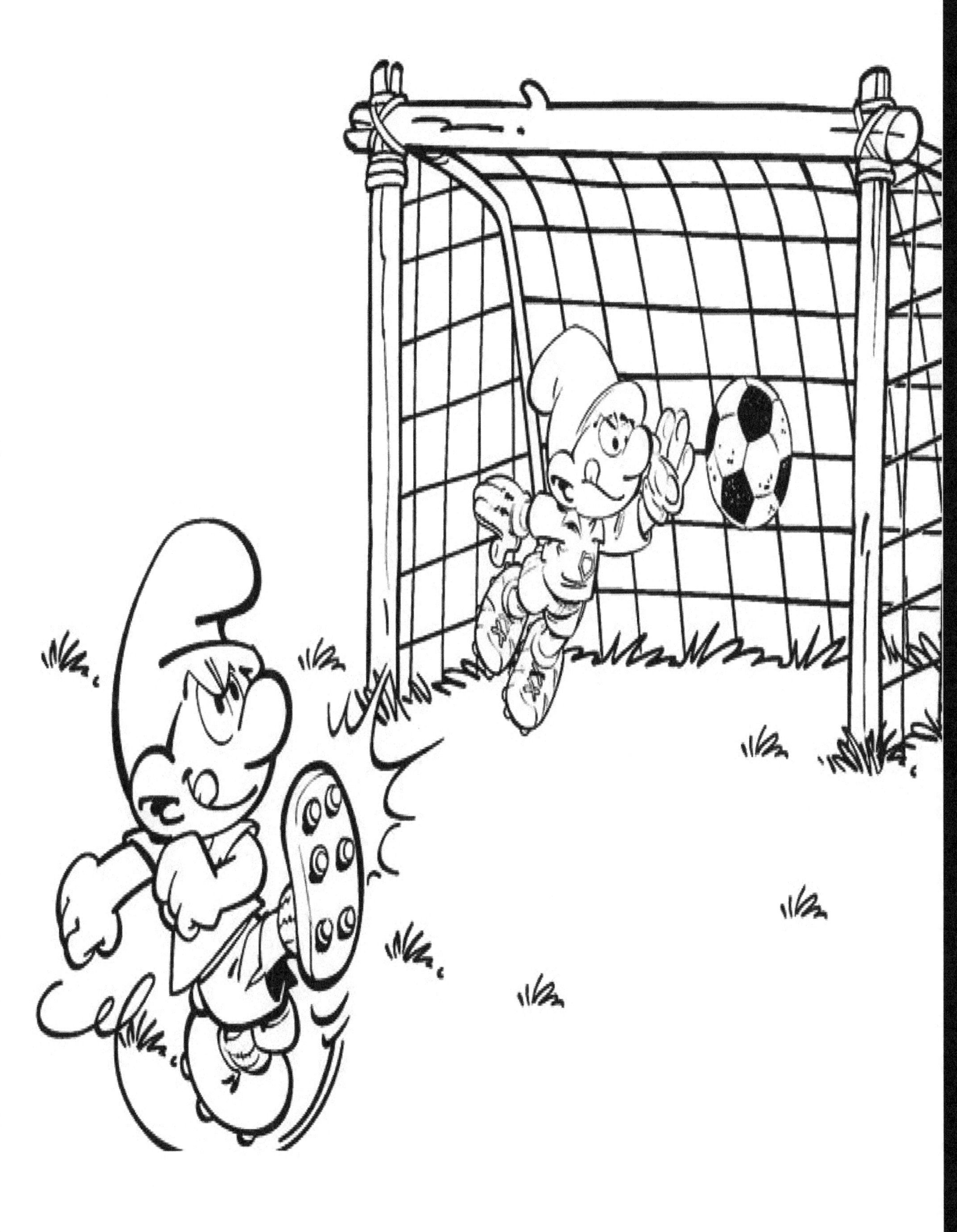

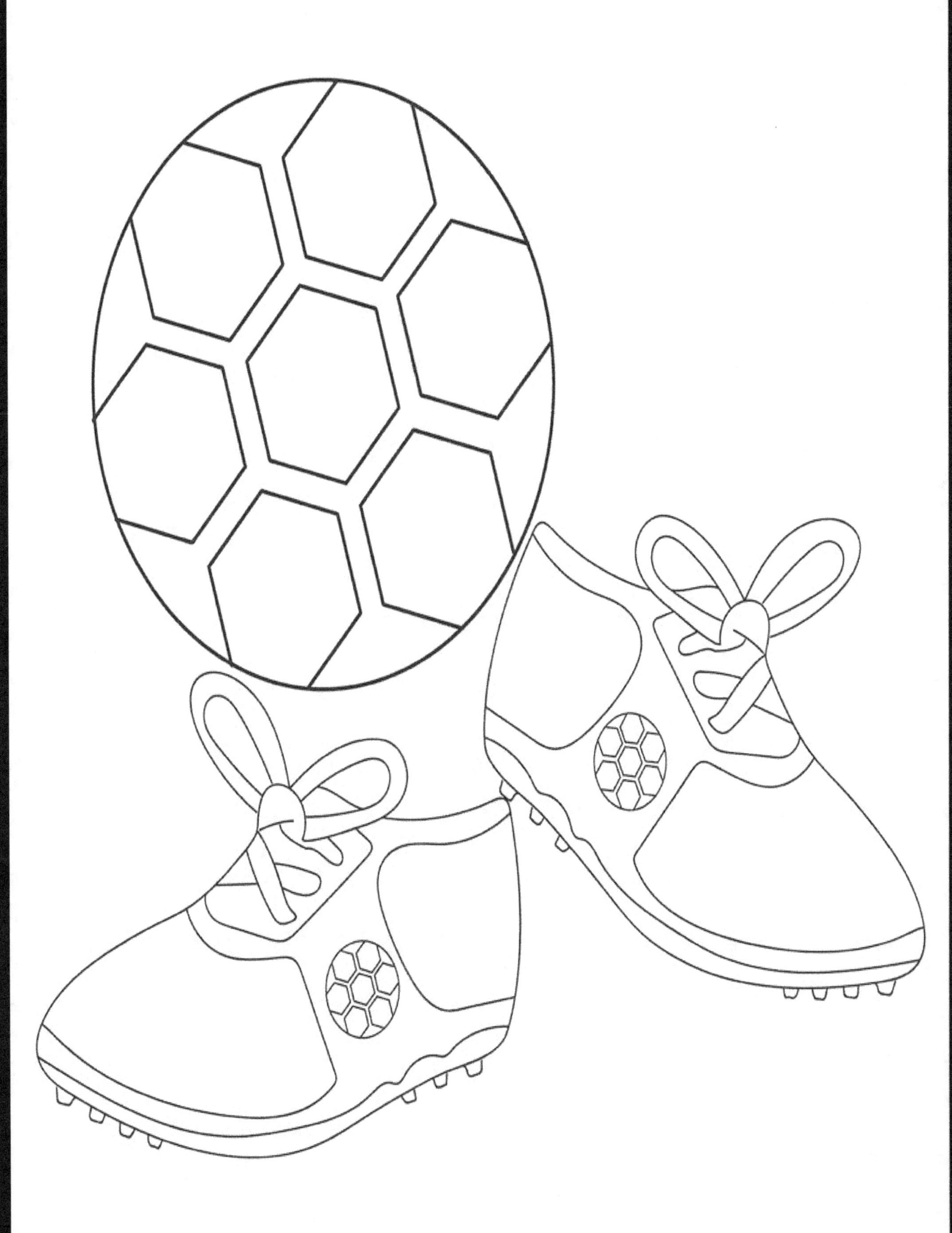

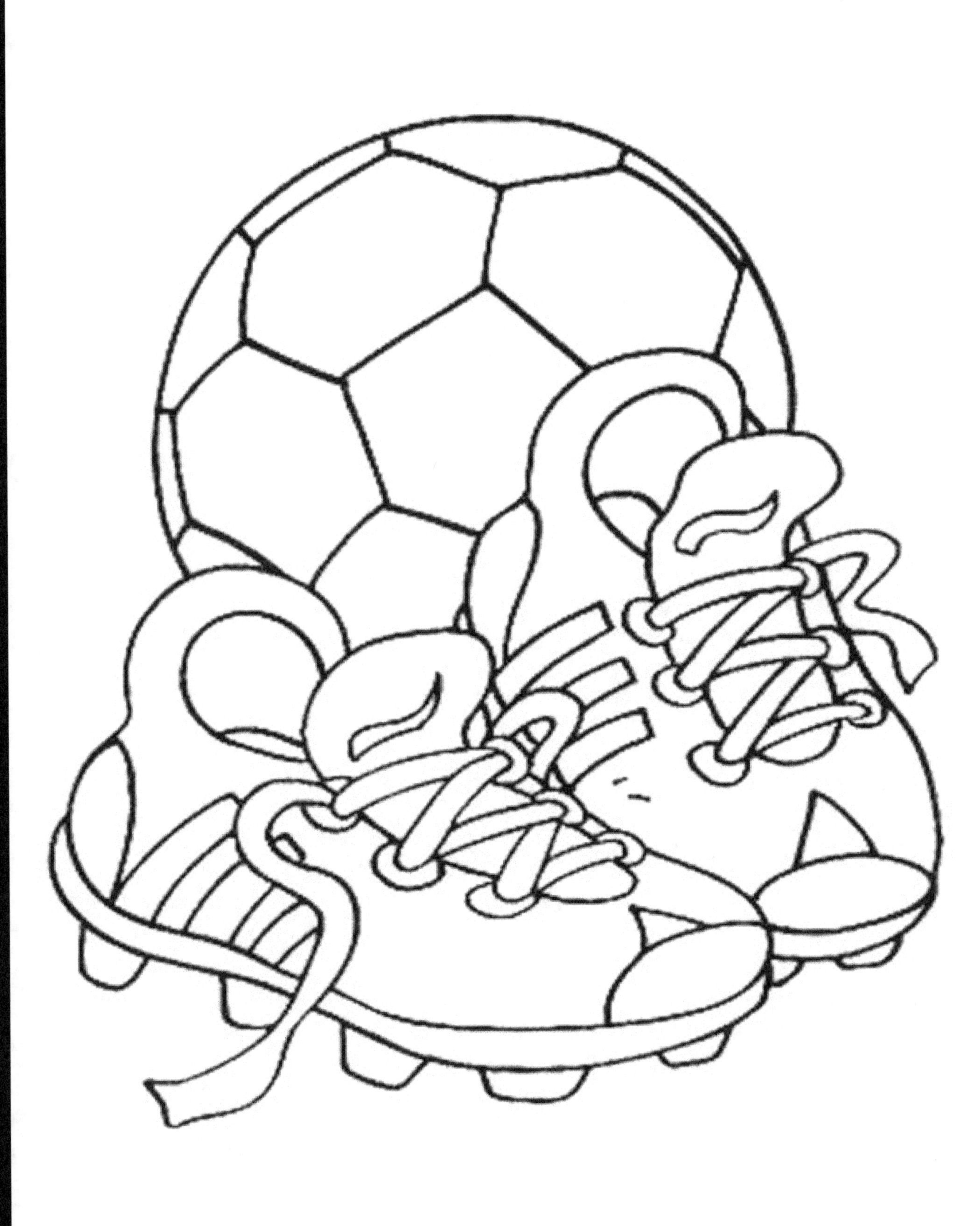

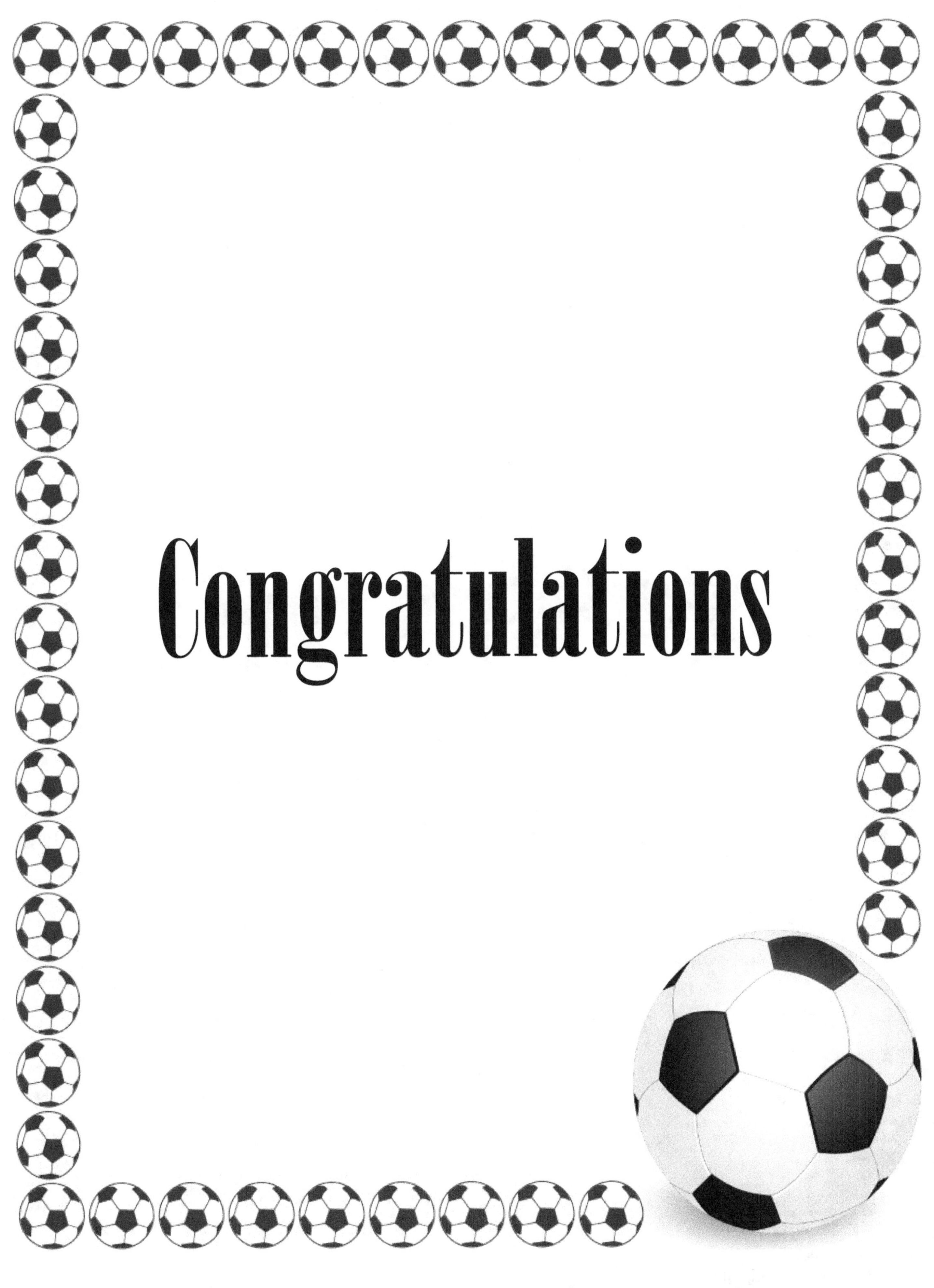
Congratulations

www.ingramcontent.com/pod-product-compliance
Lightning Source LLC
Chambersburg PA
CBHW081427250726
48654CB00013B/1852

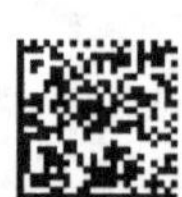
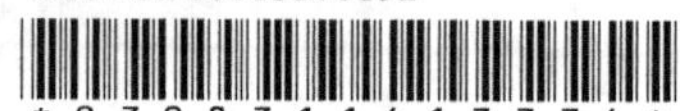